AF338258

The Battle for the Divinity of Christ in the Early Centuries

The Battle for the Divinity of Christ in the Early Centuries

Christopher Raoul Carranza

RESOURCE *Publications* · Eugene, Oregon

THE BATTLE FOR THE DIVINITY OF CHRIST IN THE EARLY CENTURIES

Resource Publications
An Imprint of Wipf and Stock Publishers
199 W. 8th Ave., Suite 3
Eugene, OR 97401

www.wipfandstock.com

PAPERBACK ISBN: 978-1-6667-5759-0
HARDCOVER ISBN: 978-1-6667-5760-6
EBOOK ISBN: 978-1-6667-5761-3

03/10/23

Contents

With special thanks to my editors
Charles Edward Carranza
Roisin McAree
Phillis Parmet
Dean Mixon

1

Ancient Christianities

Today's Christianity is highly diverse with many different churches, doctrines, teachings, beliefs, practices, ethics, requirements, etc., and—most importantly—different designations about who is and who is not a biblical Christian. All of Christendom may share the same vocabulary, but how those words are defined varies widely from group to group. The fact that Islam, and especially modern radical Islam, has lumped all of Christianity into a single category has helped the Christian world to circle the wagons a little more tightly in recent years and has dampened some of the hard-core infighting. It was only a few short decades ago that Catholics and Protestants labeled each other apostates. Many Protestant groups claimed exclusivity (some still do), and there is certainly an element of truth to the accusation that Christianity is the only religion that assembles its firing squads in a circle. In spite of the genuine efforts on the part of Roman Catholics, Protestants, the Eastern Orthodox, and others to make a concerted effort to embrace their commonality rather than their contrasts, the modern Christian world is obviously divided.

It is interesting that with almost all of today's Christians reading virtually the same Old and New Testament books (with a small addition in the Catholic Bible), there is such an amazing variety of beliefs and groups that interpret things very differently. Imagine the diversity we would have right now if every potential group had dozens of different canonical books from which to choose. That was the situation in the latter part of the first century and on down through the next few centuries, and it's the primary reason that the differences between groups were far more pronounced than they are today. The New Testament was not yet codified and there were multitudes of Gospels, writings, letters, and apocalypses alleged to have been from the original apostles. The books in the current New Testament existed, but they were not yet organized into a single agreed-upon collection. Furthermore, different areas of the empire may have used only one Gospel or known of only one of the four Gospels in the New Testament today, so their views were shaped by that Gospel. For instance, since the Gospel of Matthew is the most Jewish of the four, those groups who used only that Gospel or had access only to it developed a decidedly Jewish leaning and emphasis. Those groups who used or had access only to the Gospel of Luke, the most gentile of the Gospels, not only developed a gentile leaning and emphasis in their understandings but also at times expressed blatantly anti-Semitic ideas in their writings, similar to the overtly anti-Semitic sentiments of Martin Luther some 1300 years later. This is why anti-Jewish groups throughout world history could always pluck venomous propaganda from legitimate church writings and use them to support their hateful pogroms, persecutions, and even exterminations.

Because of all of the above, early groups had so little in common that the term *Christianities* is more applicable to the realities of the time than a single designation. Men or groups would formulate a theology, gather a following, and then get very creative in validating their beliefs. Since there was no accepted canon of scriptural books like we have today, different groups would work backwards. After establishing their theology, the more upright and conscientious Christians would edit authentic apostolic writings to support their claims. For instance, the fundamentally Jewish Ebionites kept the Old Testament and added their own edited version of Matthew's Gospel. Since they accepted that Jesus was the Jewish Messiah but denied that he was anything more than a normal man born in the normal way, they deleted the first couple of chapters of Matthew (virgin birth and such) and, of course, rejected everything that Paul wrote. The Marcionites, the Ebionites' polar opposite, believed that Jesus represented the only true God and therefore used no Old Testament books, only ten or so edited chapters from the book of Luke, and edited versions of most of Paul's letters.

You're probably thinking that all this cut-and-paste selective editing doesn't sound very upright and conscientious. It probably wasn't, except when compared to the Gnostics. The Gnostics believed that they were a chosen group, born with the divine spark, and that they had exclusive possession of secret knowledge (which is what their name means). In light of this, the Gnostics felt entitled to take extreme liberties in propagating their spiritually discerned truths. They wrote books interfused with their vocabulary and dogma, but in the style of genuine apostolic writings, and then falsely ascribed to them some weighty New Testament names. Most of their writings were penned much later than the volumes that would become the current twenty-seven New Testament books. Among their pseudepigraphical books are titles such as the Gospel of Mary Magdalene, the Gospel of Judas (which paints Judas as a "helper" of Jesus, with similar overtones to how he's portrayed in *Jesus Christ Superstar*), the Prayer of the Apostle Paul, the Secret Book of James, the Gospel of Thomas, the Gospel of Philip, the Apocalypse of Paul, the Apocalypse of James, the Gospel of Truth, the Acts of Peter and the Twelve Apostles, the Letter of Peter to Philip—and many other fabricated writings endorsing their theology.

There were many, many other sects and groups claiming to be Christian at the end of the first century, but these three were the main competitors of what would later become orthodoxy (termed *proto-orthodoxy* by biblical scholar Bart Ehrman).[1] The beliefs of those three groups, with the addition of the beliefs of the

---

1. Ehrman, "Christians Who Would Be Jews," in *Lost Christianities*, disc 1, lect. 2, 8:28.

proto-orthodox pretty much cover the four main positions about who Jesus was. And even though a multiplicity of other positions existed at the time or developed later, their perceptions of Jesus were basically adjuncts or extensions of the teachings of these four groups. The first two chapters provide a little more clarification on the three groups that did not become orthodox. However, there are many different teachings on what these groups believed because virtually none of their original writings remain today (except in the case of the Gnostics, which I will address when I get to them individually). So, what we know about at least the first two groups is derived only from the writings of their opponents and those who hoped to expunge them. Nevertheless, scholars have been able to compare critic with critic and also cross-reference the critics with other writings and come up with a reasonably accurate overview of their general beliefs.

The Ebionites

The first group addressed will be the Ebionites, which means "the poor ones." They were a Jewish Christian movement, centered in Jerusalem, who regarded Jesus as the Messiah but rejected his divinity and his virgin birth. They insisted that it was still necessary to follow Jewish law and rites, to be a Jew, and to be circumcised before you could be a Christian. That last requirement surely limited their appeal outside of Jewish Jerusalem, where the majority were already circumcised, and was an obstacle in the wider Roman Empire. Circumcision was not a requirement of the other three competing groups, who correspondingly expanded and grew at a much greater rate than the Ebionites. The Ebionites also refused to eat with gentiles unless they had been converted to Judaism—a factor that also limited their expansion. On top of this, they were vehemently opposed to the apostle Paul, the man who is often considered the second most important figure in Christianity (besides Christ himself). Since Paul's letters directly contradicted many of their assertions, they considered him an apostate.

Much like the later monks, they embraced a life of poverty and asceticism and were said to be vegetarians. The Ebionites are the simplest of the three groups to understand, since they were basically fundamental Jews who believed that their anticipated Messiah showed up with the appearing of Christ. Where they differed most significantly from the other three groups was in their perception of who Jesus Christ was. In the Torah, Moses said that another prophet would come who was like him—which implied that Christ would be a man like Moses. Therefore, the great majority of Ebionites believed that Jesus was a normal Jewish man, just as Moses had been a normal Jewish man; that he was the actual biological son of Mary and Joseph; and that he was born in the normal human way. They rejected the concept that Jesus preexisted in any form and limited his exceptionalism to his perfect adherence to the law as he went about living a simple, natural human existence. The Ebionites ran into opposition from the Jews in Jerusalem because of the crucifixion, as most of Judaism dismissed the possibility of the Messiah being executed. A dead Messiah was incongruous with long-held Jewish expectations and messianic understandings and, admittedly, did not seem to fit with many Old Testament affirmations about the Messiah. Unfortunately, since we have none of their original writings, we know about them only by what their detractors reported, and, as with the next two groups, contradictions and misinformation abound.

According to the early writers, the Ebionites rejected the atoning death of Christ, yet at the same time considered him the perfect sacrifice and therefore felt that the Jewish sacrifices at the temple were no longer necessary. This belief put them at odds with the proto-orthodox, the temple Jews, and, of course, the apostle Paul. Their belief that you had to be a Jew in order to become a Christian was sequentially logical. They accurately stated that Jesus was the Jewish Messiah, appointed by the Jewish God in order to save the Jewish people, in fulfillment of the Jewish law. From this they concluded that Christianity had to be a purely Jewish movement. They further asserted that, because of his perfect keeping of the law and sinless devotion to God, Jesus was adopted by God at his baptism and declared to be God's son. He was later raised from the dead as a reward from God. Correspondingly, the Aramaic Gospel of Matthew that the Ebionites used begins with the baptism of Jesus and is referred to by them as "the Gospel of the Hebrews." They also used the Gospel of the Ebionites, which was a compilation of the three synoptic Gospels with the parts that contradicted their theology omitted. Other groups held this same view with different timing on when Jesus was adopted by God. While the Ebionites say that Jesus was adopted at his baptism, others say it was at his resurrection or ascension. Collectively, this view of Jesus is known as *adoptionism*. As with the next two groups, you will see similarities to the beliefs of some of today's groups. Like the Ebionites, there have always been groups contending that the God of the Old Testament, Yahweh, is the only true God, and that Christ, a created being, was promoted to divine status or adopted by God or somehow made semidivine.

The Marcionites

The next group was founded by a wealthy man from modern-day northeast Turkey named Marcion (c. AD 85–160) and was thus known as the Marcionites. Marcion had been raised in a proto-orthodox Christian home and was part of a church in the city of Sinope where his father was bishop. After voicing some theories that were inconsistent with those of his upbringing, his own father called him a heretic and kicked him out of the church. Marcion had embraced Docetism, which is derived from the Greek for "to seem" or "phantom." This theology teaches that Christ was so divine that he only seemed or appeared to be human. He was an illusion whose flesh-and-blood body was an apparition. Marcion also denied that Christ ever hungered or thirsted or suffered or died on the cross, because God did not have an actual physical body capable of suffering. Moreover, since without a body he could not possibly have been born, Marcion believed that this illusion appeared on earth completely formed as a full-grown man some time closely following the death of Emperor Augustus in AD 14.

Marcion taught that there were two distinct Gods, proposing that the "creator God" of the Old Testament was an evil inferior being and that the real God showed up only with the appearance of Christ. He argued that the vengeful, jealous, murderous God of the Old Testament, who had ordered the slaughter of every man, woman, and child in Jericho as well as the annihilation of many other native residents of Canaan, could not possibly be the same God of love and mercy portrayed in the New Testament. In his book *The Antitheses*, of which no copies remain today, Marcion goes to great lengths to show what he sees as irreconcilable differences between the "Gods" of the two Testaments. By pointing out the many contrasts between the Old and New Testament deities, he surmised that the Jewish creator God, who made this defective material world as a place of hopelessness and suffering, was a completely different entity than that higher, benevolent, transcendent God portrayed in the New Testament. He completely rejected the Old Testament except for using it as proof that the inferior creator God had an earthly human body, as he is described as walking in the garden of Eden, and also that he was so lacking in knowledge that he didn't even know where Adam was and had to call out in order to find him. The *demiurge*, the name that Marcion ascribed to the evil tribal God of the Jews, delighted in legalistic, retributive punishments and caused the unfortunate, sinful humans who inhabited his creation to suffer and die. This demiurge gave the Jews the law, chose them as his people, and then punished the entire planet for everyone's failure to keep the law. Marcion declared that the God who gave the Gospel could not be the same God who gave the law. Christ, who could be neither part of this God nor part of what he created, came to oppose this Old Testament tyrant and introduce us to the true loving God for the first time. He was also tasked with setting us free from this demiurge and from death. Marcion venerated the apostle Paul even more than the disciples who had actually been with Christ, and he considered him the only apostle who had been given the mysterious knowledge of the true message of the Gospel. Justin Martyr (c. AD 100–165), who coincidentally happened to be in Rome at the same time as Marcion, did not quote from Paul's letters in any of his writings. Historians believe that his omission of Paul's letters was done to counter the Marcionites; they conjecture that any mention of them would have been seen as an endorsement of Marcion's highly edited versions in which all references to the Old Testament were erased. Justin Martyr vehemently opposed Marcion, so this conjecture may have some merit. In his arguments, Justin did quote extensively from the current four Gospels without citing them specifically.

In comparing the Ebionites to the Marcionites, it becomes clear why they were considered the polar opposite of each other. The first worshipped the God of the Old Testament; the second, the God of the New Testament. The first carefully followed the Old Testament and kept the law, while the second rejected both. The first saw Christ as a man and not God, while the second saw him as God and not a man. Finally, the Ebionites rejected everything that Paul had written, while the Marcionites considered him the only complete and true apostle. While there were other contrasts, the above examples are sufficient to show some of the opposing characteristics of these two groups.

It's unfortunate that none of Marcion's actual writings exist today, because he was a clever thinker, talented writer, and convincing speaker. How convincing? After leaving his home town, he journeyed to Rome around AD 139 and joined the Christian community there. After a few years of using his wealth to make large donations to the Roman Christian community and thereby solidifying his connections, he called the very first Christian council in AD 144 in an attempt to make his teachings the official Christian doctrine in Rome. As if that wasn't bold and innovative enough, he is credited with putting forth the first Christian canon, consisting of his ten edited chapters of Luke and most of the letters of Paul (highly edited, of course). Marcion's first closed canon inspired the proto-orthodox to speed up the process of putting forth an agreed-upon canon of their own, which was not officially established until AD 367 by Athanasius. However, as mentioned earlier, before presenting the letters of Paul in his "Bible," Marcion removed all the places where Paul talked about the Old Testament and the fulfillment of Old Testament prophecies, which later prompted Tertullian's (c. AD 155–240) famous quip: "Marcion interpreted these books with a penknife."[2] Just like today's theological outliers, Marcion claimed it necessary to edit legitimate Scripture because others had corrupted its original form, or inferior minds had failed to understand what they had mistakenly written.

Marcion's charisma and intellect were such that he easily garnered converts, and even those who opposed him paid him a backhanded compliment by singling him out as the "arch-heretic" of the second century. Polycarp (c. AD 65–155), the disciple of the apostle John, who had been appointed bishop of Smyrna by John, also happened to be visiting Rome at the same time that Marcion was there. He saw the man and his doctrine as a serious threat to the apostle John's Christianity and called Marcion "the firstborn of Satan."[3] Others in the council must have regarded him similarly, as they rejected both his premise and his bible and promptly kicked him out of the Church of Rome. But, ever the survivor, Marcion retreated to his home area back in Sinope and, employing his substantial intellectual and dialectic skills, was very successful in spreading his doctrine and building his churches. He was so successful, in fact, that vast areas of Asia Minor were converted to his theology, and there remained whole Marcionite villages and churches well into the fourth and fifth centuries.

Interestingly, one of Marcion's fundamental premises lives on today and, unlike modern-day Ebionite remnants, is not limited to a small minority of Christians. While many Christians loosely echo the periphery of Marcion's tenets when speaking of the contrast between Old Testament demands and New Testament grace, and still others reduce the Old Testament to a second-class category or ignore it completely, one of Marcion's essential teachings dominates mainstream Christianity and is continually propagated through mainstream Christian media. Marcion's premise that Paul had "secret knowledge" that the other apostles did not have

2. Ehrman, "Christians Who Refuse to Be Jews," in *Lost Christianities*, disc 1, lect. 3, 26:05.

3. Jackson, *Early Church Classics*, 10.

is the basis of the entire dispensational system that promotes the rapture and many of the modern-day mainstream teachings. An anti-Marcion rebuke of the premise from the late second century may still merit some consideration today, since only books from our current New Testament were quoted in this condemnation:

> With regard to those [the Marcionites] who allege that Paul alone knew the truth, and that to him the mystery was manifested by revelation, let Paul himself convict them, when he says, that one and the same God [made Peter the apostle of the Jews, and Paul the apostle of] the Gentiles. Peter, therefore, was an apostle of [the same God as] was Paul; and Him whom Peter preached as God among [the Jews] . . . did Paul [preach] among the Gentiles. For our Lord never came to save Paul alone, nor is God so limited in means, that He should have but one apostle who knew the dispensation of His Son. And again, when Paul says, "How beautiful are the feet of those bringing glad tidings of good things, and preaching the Gospel of peace," he shows clearly that it was not merely one, but there were many who used to preach the truth. And again, in the Epistle to the Corinthians, when he had recounted all those who had seen God after the resurrection, he says in continuation, "But whether it was I or they so we preach, and so ye believed," acknowledging as one and the same, the preaching of all those who saw God after the resurrection from the dead.[4]

This second-century writer is affirming the fact that both Paul and Peter taught the exact same truths. It is also noteworthy that Paul's own words castigate anyone who asserts otherwise ("let Paul himself convict them").

Further down in the paragraph, excerpts from two of Paul's New Testament letters are cited in order to confirm that, besides Peter, other apostles taught and preached the same truths as Paul had declared. He continues:

> If Paul had known any mysteries unrevealed to the other apostles, Luke, his constant companion and

4. Irenaeus, *Against Heresies*, bk 3, 436.

fellow-traveler could not have been ignorant of them; neither could the truth possibly [have been hidden] from him, through whom alone we learn many and most important particulars of the Gospel history. But that this Luke was inseparable from Paul, and his fellow-laborer in the gospel, he himself clearly evidences, not as a matter of boasting, but is bound to do by the truth itself.[5]

The writer emphasizes the unique closeness and communion between Paul and Luke. It is therefore inconceivable that any "mysteries" that Paul would have openly shared with recently converted pagans would not first have been shared with (and certainly overheard by) "his fellow-laborer in the gospel." He then draws our attention to Luke's passion for divulging every facet of what he had absorbed, by quoting many of his finer details from the book of Acts, such as sailing from Troas towards Samothracia, the rest of their journey as far as Philippi, and how they delivered their first address:

> "For sitting down," [Luke says], "we spake onto the women who had assembled; and many believed . . ." And all the remaining [details] of this course with Paul he recounts, indicating with all diligence both places, and cities, and number of days, until they went up to Jerusalem; and what befell Paul there, how he was sent to Rome in bonds; the name of the centurion who took him in charge; and the signs of the ships [and their shipwreck; and the name of the island upon which they escaped].
>
> As Luke was present at all these occurrences, he carefully noted them down in writing, so that he cannot be convicted of falsehood or boastfulness, because all these [particulars] prove both that he was senior to all those who now teach otherwise, and that he was not ignorant of the truth. That he was not merely a follower, but a fellow-laborer of the apostles, but especially of Paul. . . . He was always attached to and inseparable from him. And again, he says, in the Epistle to the Colossians: "Luke, the beloved physician, greets you." But surely Luke, who always preached in company with Paul, and is

---

5. Irenaeus, *Against Heresies*, bk 3, 437.

called by him "the beloved," and with him performed the work of an evangelist, and was entrusted to hand down to us a Gospel, learned nothing different from [Paul], as has been pointed out from his words, how can these men, who were never attached to Paul, boast that they have learned hidden and unspeakable mysteries?

But that Paul taught with simplicity what he knew, not only to those who were [employed] with him, but those that heard him, he does himself make manifest . . . [Paul], referring to the evil teachers who should arise, said: "I know that after my departure shall grievous wolves come to you, not sparing the flock. Also, of your own selves shall men arise, speaking perverse things, to draw away disciples after them." "I have not shunned," he says "to declare unto you all the counsel of God . . ." Now if any man set Luke aside, as one who did not know the truth, he will [by so acting] manifestly reject the Gospel of which he claims to be a disciple. For through him we have become acquainted with very many and important parts of the Gospel.[6]

Irenaeus, the disciple of Polycarp (who was himself a disciple of the apostle John), wrote the above statement in about AD 180. He distinctly rebukes the Marcionite claim back then—or anyone's claim today—that Paul alone knew any secret truth that other apostles did not. He also seems quite certain that the meticulously detail-oriented Luke, Paul's "constant companion and fellow-traveler could not have been ignorant of [everything Paul taught in their travels together]; neither could the truth possibly [have been hidden] from him."[7] There will be much more on this remarkable man in the final chapter of this book.

6. Irenaeus, *Against Heresies*, bk 3, 437.

7. Irenaeus, *Against Heresies*, bk 3, 438.

2

The Gnostics

Just as there are clearly recognizable theological remnants from the above two groups circulating in the Christian community today, there are also remnants from the group that will be addressed next. The Gnostics have a loose connection to some aspects of modern Christianity because of the sheer volume of their writings and the recent documentation that divulges a wide spectrum of beliefs. While the previous two groups have a recognizable presence today because of their specificity and relatively concise teachings, the Gnostics have a peripheral presence because of their confused and often contradictory writings. Their writings are so broad that there was even a renewal of interest in a more secular, philosophical form of Gnosticism in the twentieth century that attracted people such as the famous psychologist Carl Jung. However, their most enduring legacy is probably their successful church growth formula, which played on human pride, exclusivity, elitism, the authority of one's own spiritual self-assessment, and eternal guarantees, which has been successfully employed down through the millennia and lives on today.

The Gnostics, like the Marcionites, were dualistic—that is, believing in opposing Gods, with the evil God being inferior to the good God. This dualism is contradictory to both Jewish and

Christian belief systems in which, as Maimonides and many others understood, evil has no separate existence. Unlike both the Ebionites and the Marcionites, we do have original writings from the Gnostics, thanks to the 1945 discovery of the Nag Hammadi Library in Egypt.

A local farmer discovered a buried, sealed jar containing multiple codices believed to have been written during the third or fourth centuries. Contained within the codices were over fifty different compositions all written in the Coptic language. This find turned out to be a treasure trove of early Gnostic writings explaining some of their beliefs and tenets. However, since it was written for the Gnostic believers themselves, many of the finer points of their theology were left out because it was assumed that the faithful already knew the basics. Moreover, as explained in the documentary series *Ancient Roads from Christ to Constantine*, it's very difficult to define Gnosticism because of all its various groups, diverse fragmentations, and independent beliefs. When asked what the Gnostics believed, Dr. Rebecca Lyman hit the nail on the head when she replied: "That's a highly contested question. . . . You might see these as people in these communities that didn't necessarily have strict boundaries, doing different exegesis on the Bible stories and writing different accounts."[1]

Before the discovery of the Nag Hammadi Library, historians had a relatively uniform, though in some respects inaccurate, understanding of the Gnostics. Their detractors had been fairly consistent in their condemnation of perceived Gnostic beliefs, because many of the later critics read and incorporated the writings of earlier critics before penning their own original thoughts. Collectively, they may have been reasonably accurate in regard to Valentinian Gnosticism, the most prevalent form that existed in the second and third centuries, but that's not the whole story. As it turns out, other forms of Gnosticism may predate Christ. Although no pre-Christian Gnostic writings have yet been found, there appear to be both pre-Christian and post-Christian forms of

---

1. Rebecca Lyman, in Phillips, "From Apocalypse To Heresies," in *Ancient Roads*, disc 2, lect. 1, 3:14.

Gnosticism. The first is focused on the Jewish Scriptures, and there are known to be Gnostic commentaries on the first six chapters of Genesis and other writings that intertwined Gnosticism with Judaism. Later, their post-Christian writings intertwined the prevalent Valentinian Gnosticism with Christianity by making Christ a uniquely constructed offspring of the female spirit being Sophia. As the *Encyclopedia of Philosophy* states,

> Irenaeus, who was writing only about five years after the death of Valentinus, and in whose treatise *Against Heresies* the outline of Valentinus' cosmology is preserved, [says] the entity responsible for initiating the drama is referred to simply as "the mother," by which is probably meant Sophia (Wisdom). From this "mother" both matter (*hulê*) and the savior, Christ, were generated.[2]

Their "Christ," in concert with their theology, became incarnate to bring gnosis ("secret knowledge") to the earth. Because of the lack of "strict boundaries" in their writings, there were also other Gnostic views of Christ that will be touched upon later. After the discovery of the Nag Hammadi Library, historians discovered the truth of the adage "Be careful what you wish for," as the 1945 discovery led to more questions than answers and more disagreement and controversy than historical agreement. However, in spite of the ongoing debates and the plethora of contradictory information, their basic system, which the proto-orthodox had extensively written against, did come into sharper focus with the discovery of the Gnostics' own words.

While anyone would be on shaky ground in asserting that he or she could state exactly what the Gnostics, as a whole, believed, there is an accepted overview that most historians would agree upon in general terms. However, calling the Gnostics a Christian group is a misnomer. They were not a singular group with a singular theology, but rather many different groups, at many different times and with many different beliefs. In the late 1980s scholars began to point out that "Gnosticism" might be too broad a category

2. Moore, "Gnosticism."

for meaningful assertions about it.[3] With the discovery of the Nag Hammadi Library, many scholars are currently debating whether they can even be called "Christian," because, as some scholars have stated, Gnostic foundational beliefs sound more like the ancient Greek religions than the Christian religion. This is not surprising, since many experts claim that Gnosticism sprang from Iranian and Mesopotamian influences or from Syrian-Egyptian traditions.

The very name *Gnosticism* is derived from the Greek, meaning "having knowledge," or "being one of the knowledgeable ones." Their contemporary critics, of course, found them smug and conceited for defining themselves as the only ones who had the secret knowledge and the truth about God. Reciprocally, they themselves found all other groups ignorant, precisely because these others lacked the secret knowledge and the truth about God. It's patently clear that "orthodoxy" (from the Greek, meaning "right opinion") was in the eye of the beholder, as was "heresy." Of course, the same is true today, as no group sees itself as heretical. If any group did consider its theology heretical, it could easily remedy the situation by embracing a more accurate theology than the one currently held, which is something that groups rarely do. This is why the clarifications and conditions in the New Testament writings are rarely applied honestly and effectively. Every group views the statements that apply to true believers and heaven as relevant to their group and, conversely, all the statements that apply to being misled and deceived as relevant to other groups. That's followed by circular logic in which groups claim that they themselves are the true believers while others are merely professing believers; therefore, all of the positive biblical words are meant for them and their theological compatriots. As was true back then and is equally true today, group pride renders the New Testament conditions and safeguards difficult, if not impossible, to be used as intended.

That being said, second-century Gnostics generally believed in some form of a supreme Godhead or Monad. This true God was all spirit and therefore completely unknown and unknowable by the inhabitants of the created order. Because we are sensate and

3. See "Gnosticism" for further information.

comprehend things through sight, sound, smell, and touch, we are incapable of perceiving anything about this pure Spiritual Being. Our brains cannot even begin to understand this Monad, since it, like the rest of our bodies, is material. (Up to this point in the paragraph, the Gnostics don't sound terribly atypical.)

However, emanating from this supreme Godhead were numerous lower gods called aeons, who, together with this Godhead, comprised the elite spiritual realm that they called the heavenly *pleroma*, or "fullness." There was some kind of divine catastrophe in the heavenly pleroma that resulted in one of the aeons (called Sophia by some) conceiving an evil emanation, and that emanation created this evil physical world. Although everything in the created order was hopelessly evil, traces of the true divinity, called the *divine spark*, cascaded from the heavens and were internally locked within chosen human beings. This spark could be recognized and liberated only by *gnosis*, which was divine intuitive knowledge transmitted in a purely spiritual way. This secret knowledge was unavailable to our human senses; only a divine emissary, in this case, Christ, could come down and impart the knowledge to set the sparks free. As with almost everything in Gnosticism, there was a schism in Gnostic beliefs regarding the person of Jesus Christ. First, the name Jesus Christ can't even be used because the Valentinian Gnostics saw Christ and Jesus as two different entities. Jesus, they say, was up on the cross, but Christ had left him prior to the crucifixion and therefore was not on the cross. As mentioned earlier, most Valentinian Gnostics saw Christ as a unique emanation from the male-female aspects of Godhead. Thus, by this understanding, Christ was neither God nor man. Valentinus, adhering to the tenets of virtually all Gnostics, taught that there were many divine aeons, but he believed that Christ was distinctive. Other Gnostics believed that Christ was not a unique aeon, but simply one of the many divine aeons. A small minority claimed that Jesus Christ, a singular entity, was a mere mortal who was endowed with the divine spark, through which he attained divinity by gnosis and was therefore both an example and aim for them.[4]

4. Brons, "Brief Summary."

Delving deeply into as many Gnostic sources as possible results not in clarity, but rather a headache. For example, the Gnostic Society Library calls the Superior Monad an aeon and doesn't even get around to Christ until late in the chain of aeons. It says: "From this first being, also an Aeon, a series of different emanations occur, beginning in certain Gnostic texts with Barbelo, from which successive pairs of Aeons emanate, often in male-female pairings. . . . Two of the most commonly paired aeons were Christ and Sophia."[5] Many sources try to avoid the extreme Gnostic fringes in an attempt to stay centered, yet confusion abounds. College professors and authors, paid to present unique, new, and interesting views, are all over the map when it comes to Gnosticism. That's because any trajectory one wishes to take can probably be justified by focusing on specific, handpicked Gnostic writings, as those twentieth-century secular philosophers (mentioned earlier) were able to do.

However, the purpose here is not to define every form of Gnosticism or to condense it into a singular theosophy, but to give an overview of one of the prevalent theologies competing with proto-orthodoxy during the first few centuries of the Christian era. In his *History of the Church* (written in the fourth century), Eusebius gives the impression that proto-orthodoxy was the dominant norm and that all these other groups were minor players in the background. Most experts now see Eusebius not as a writer of history but as a rewriter of history, as these groups were far more prevalent and influential than he reports. Even the backlash against these groups at the time shows that they were a force that had to be reckoned with. The ultimate victory of the proto-orthodox was not the foregone conclusion Eusebius makes it out to be. There was a legitimate battle raging, and at stake was the very nature of Christianity.

It must also be noted that even Valentinian Gnosticism, generally regarded as the most Christian form, still contained most of these unfamiliar Gnostic aspects. Because of that, the argument by some modern historians that Gnosticism was not a form of

5. Brons, "Brief Summary."

Christianity may be valid. This is especially true if Valentius's personal history, as written by his contemporaries, is true. It's widely reported that Valentinus, a native of Alexandria, journeyed to Rome in the early 130s and was there at about the same time as Marcion and some of the others who have been mentioned. He may initially have been closer in theology to the proto-orthodox, as his detractors tell us that he was almost elected bishop of Rome. The same people say that his disappointment at not being elected caused him to shift his beliefs radically and to embrace Gnosticism. The Gnostic Society Library, a modern group, says that

> Valentinus believed that God is androgynous and frequently depicted him as a male-female dyad.... The male and female aspects of the father, acting in conjunction, manifested themselves in the Son. The Son is also often depicted by the Valentinians as a male-female dyad. ... The Valentinian tradition draws a sharp distinction between the human Jesus and the divine Jesus. The human Jesus was born the true son of Mary and Joseph. By a special dispensation, his body is co-substantial with Sophia and her spiritual seed.[6]

If his detractors are correct in regard to his attempt to become bishop, then maybe they are also right about his radical shift, as it seems unlikely that someone holding the above views (male/female Father and Son, Sophia, etc.) would have been considered a viable candidate for the office of bishop of Rome.

The Gnostic position on salvation is a little more uniform and easier to follow than their teachings on Christ. Basically, "gnosis is mystical or esoteric knowledge based on direct participation with the divine. In most Gnostic systems, the sufficient cause of salvation is this 'knowledge of' ('acquaintance with') the divine. It is an inward 'knowing.'"[7] Therefore, true Gnostics would have secret knowledge of the innate internal spark and their intimate involvement with the divinity. They themselves would become

6. See Brons, "Brief Summary."

7. Ehrman, "Early Gnostic Christianity—Our Sources," in *Lost Christianities*, disc 1, lect. 4, 3:40.

aware of and know for sure that they were part of the divine realm. By virtue of being a member of the very highest human category, they would be entitled to the supreme form of salvation.

It's generally believed that Gnostics understood there to be three categories of human beings. The first category was the animal nature human beings. These were pure material beings and were just like other animals that only seemed to be alive or were only materially alive. These "animals" were created simply to be snuffed out and had no more value than an ant. The second category was comprised of believing Christians, some of whom were being martyred, while others were widely recognized throughout the Roman Empire for their unique charitable works. The social gospel of helping the downtrodden was a novelty in a society where between one quarter and one-third of the Roman population served as slaves. Not that the wealthy Romans didn't give to the less fortunate, but it was more for the edification, image, and potential social and/or political benefit of the giver. The Gnostics recognized that there would be a type of afterlife for these exemplary people based on their faith and works. They had "earned" some semblance of a positive afterlife; however, because they were lacking the divine spark, they were outside of the criteria for the supreme spiritual afterlife. That elite afterlife was reserved for the Gnostics alone who, after a maturing of the divine spark, would have acquired enough of the secret knowledge to know for certain who they really were. While the believing Christians would enjoy some kind of positive afterlife, possibly on a rejuvenated earth, the Gnostics alone would rise into the pleroma and live in the presence of the Supreme Monad. From their writings, some historians have suggested that various aeons were in charge of different levels of the upper atmosphere and that part of the secret knowledge was a series of passwords that would be necessary to move on through the various levels. But, as with almost everything concerning Gnosticism, other experts disagree.

Interestingly, the Gnostics, like the Marcionites, also found the writings of Paul very useful in supporting their theology. Paul's writings are complicated; and obviously, the more complicated the writing, the more subject it is to self-promoting interpretation. Peter warned that "[Paul's] letters contain some things that are hard to understand, which ignorant and unstable people distort, as they do other Scriptures, to their own destruction" (2 Pet 3:16 NIV). Just as Justin Martyr omitted Paul's letters from his own writings because of how the Marcionites had been using them, author James Dunn states that Tertullian later called Paul "the apostle of the heretics," because of how the Gnostics had been using his words. He goes on to say that "Paul's writings were attractive to the Gnostics [when] interpreted in the Gnostic way." Paul described the Corinthian church members as "having knowledge."[8] He goes on to imply that the Gnostics took these favorably worded verses as an affirmation of their beliefs. It's very easy to understand how the Gnostics could have seen the places where Paul mentions *knowledge* as an overt reference to their group. It would be similar to how many modern-day Jehovah's Witnesses think it a personal reference when the word *witnesses* appears in the Bible (as in Isa 43:10 NIV: "You are my witnesses"). Paul used the buzzwords *knowledge* and *know* in many verses, and the Gnostics easily personalized and took advantage of those particular Scriptures, including many like the ones below:

- Rom 10:2: "Their [enemies'] zeal is not based on knowledge."

- Rom 11:33: "Oh, the depth of the riches of wisdom and knowledge"

- Rom 15:14: "You yourselves are full of goodness, filled with knowledge and competent to instruct one another."

- 1 Cor 1:5: "For in him you have been enriched in every way— with all kinds of speech and with all knowledge"

- 1 Cor 8:7: "But not everyone possesses this knowledge."

- 1 Cor 12:8: "To one there is given through the spirit a message of wisdom, to another a message of knowledge by means of the same spirit"

8. Dunn, "Apostle of the Heretics," 208.

- 2 Cor 2:14: "[God] uses us to spread the aroma of the knowledge"

- 2 Cor 10:5: "We demolish arguments and every pretension that sets itself up against the knowledge of God"

- 2 Cor 11:6: "I may indeed be untrained as a speaker, but I do have knowledge."

And there are many more such "knowledge" references throughout Paul's writings.

Armed with some of the fabricated apostolic writings previously mentioned, in addition to his own truncated Bible (that highlighted Paul's apparent endorsement of his theology), Valentinus left Rome after his failed bid to become bishop. Even in an age without mass media, he was still able to rapidly spread his Gnosticism throughout northwest Africa, Egypt, and even as far away as Syria and Asia Minor. Unsurprisingly, his Gnosticism garnered an impressive following by appealing to human pride and vanity. His contemporary critics pointed out how smug and conceited the elitist Valentinus and his self-righteous followers were, and he appears to have had little difficulty convincing potential converts that they were uniquely exceptional people who were "called" and "glorified" and personally given "the gift of knowing [the Father] by the power of the Logos."[9] Valentinus continued his church growth spiel by telling his listeners that they were the very ones "whose name the Father has pronounced" and that "the Father 'knows the things that are yours, so that you may rest yourselves in them.'"[10] He capped off his appeal by guaranteeing that they could "know" for sure that they are "from above."[11]

The Old Testament shows that the false teachers and false prophets used a similar type of easily digested flattery with great success, as do some today. Furthermore, what made the Gnostic proselytizing even more irresistible and their exponential growth inevitable was the fact that it was all based upon the potential

9. Barnstone, *Other Bible*, 291, 294, 297.

10. Barnstone, *Other Bible*, 291.

11. Barnstone, *Other Bible*, 292.

converts' own self-assessment. As written in the Gospel of Truth, their primary book (said to be written by Valentinus himself): "After all these came also the little children, those who possess the knowledge of the Father. . . . They came to know and they were known. . . . Hence, if one has knowledge, he is from above. If he is called, he hears, he replies and he turns toward him who called him and he ascends to heaven and he knows what he is called. Since he has knowledge."[12]

Gnostics proclaimed that the culmination of secret knowledge reached its pinnacle when you came to know who you really are (a preordained, heaven-bound spirit trapped in a human body) and when you yourself affirmed the invisible, incomprehensible, absolute knowledge of your real self. The Valentinian Gnostics capitalized on the fact that this cleverly crafted theology was very difficult to counter because genuine Scripture "proved" the validity of the converts' own self-assessment. Every time Paul used the word *know* or *knowledge*, it was not only an exclusive reference to all Gnostics but also an unassailable affirmation of every Gnostic's eternal place with the Father. Thus, as a Gnostic, you could "know" with certainty that you were one of the chosen of God, indwelt with his divine spark, and certain to be one of those who ascends to heaven.

As mentioned at the outset of this chapter, the above paragraph may sound strikingly familiar because of its unmistakable parallel with many of today's modern Christian messages. These modern messages are designed, as were the Gnostic messages, in the interest of popular appeal and church growth. More eerily, wording and utilization that are similar to those of the Gnostics are still used today—or more to the point, misused, in order to pander to human pride, exclusivity, elitism, the authority of one's own spiritual self-assessment, and the handing out of eternal guarantees, with scriptural-sounding justifications.

Just as some do today, Valentinus fed his audience a string of rhetorical questions that virtually no one, in their own self-assessment, could answer in the negative. In the following excerpts from the Gospel of Truth, he asks if they personally believe that they

12. Barnstone, *Other Bible*, 292.

love and know the truth, are joined with the Holy Spirit, know the Father and the Son, are in the light, and whether they consider themselves God's children.

The Gospel of Truth says:

> For each one loves truth because truth is the mouth of the Father. His tongue is the Holy Spirit, who joins him to truth.[13]

> He gave them the means of knowing the knowledge of the Father and the revelation of his son. . . . Say then in your heart that you are this perfect day and that in you the light which does not fail dwells.[14]

> Do not be a place of the devil, for you have already destroyed him.[15]

> Such are they who possess from above something of this immeasurable greatness, as they strain towards that unique and perfect one who exists there for them. And they do not go down to Hades. They have neither envy nor moaning, nor is death in them. But they rest in him who rests, without wearying themselves or becoming involved in the search for truth. But, they, indeed, are the truth, and the Father is in them, and they are in the Father, since they are perfect, inseparable from him who is truly good. They lack nothing in any way, but they are given rest and are refreshed by the Spirit. And they listen to their root; they have leisure for themselves, they in whom he will find his root, and he will suffer no loss to his soul.[16]

> The Father is good. And his children are perfect and worthy of his name, because he is the Father. Children of this kind are those whom he loves.[17]

13. Barnstone, *Other Bible*, 293.
14. Barnstone, *Other Bible*, 294.
15. Barnstone, *Other Bible*, 294.
16. Barnstone, *Other Bible*, 297.
17. Barnstone, *Other Bible*, 297.

Valentinus used his own Gospel of Truth and not unedited genuine Scripture, because his message and guarantees would have been challenged by the qualifications and admonishments that are ubiquitous throughout the New Testament. As the late John Gerstner writes, "All Paul's letters are to professing Christians, some of whom are genuine and some of whom are not. In 2 Corinthians 13:5 he asks these professing Christians to examine themselves to see which they are, and he regularly does the same in his other letters. . . . Paul never assumes that all his readers were converted persons."[18] All of the New Testament is written to professing Christians; as such, Valentinus or any preacher could not legitimately use the verses where one is said to know something and apply it to everyone listening, or everyone who simply reads that verse.

So, it's now obvious why the Gnostic message spread like wildfire and not only was highly successful and popular, but also, along with the Marcionites, posed a formidable, almost back-breaking challenge to the proto-orthodox. In chapters 1 and 2, the Ebionite, Marcionite, and Gnostic points of view on the nature of Christ have been dealt with. In the next chapter I will examine the fourth group, the proto-orthodox, and their position that Jesus is God.

18. Gertsner, *Wrongly Dividing*, 349.

3

The Proto-Orthodox

Closest to the Fountainhead

THE PROTO-ORTHODOX POSITION BECAME the fundamental orthodoxy that most of us are familiar with today. The Italian Ravenna Church (consecrated in AD 547) gives an oversimplified explanation of the position to all education levels of that time. There is a painting of Jesus as a young man, followed by a painting of a lamb, culminating with the painting of a bearded Jesus on a throne. It's graphically saying that Jesus is fully a man, that Jesus is the Lamb that takes away the sin of the world, and that Jesus is fully God. This was the proto-orthodox position and, of course, has been the orthodox position for some 1,600 years.

During the first and second centuries, the proto-orthodox shared at least some christological commonality with two of their three contemporaries. They agreed with the Ebionites that Jesus Christ was fully man but disagreed when they said he was not God. They agreed with the Marcionites that Jesus Christ was fully God but disagreed when they said he was not a man. Finally, they shared little common ground with the Gnostics because the starting point for any meaningful dialogue would involve dividing Christ and Jesus into separate entities and then choosing from multitudes of Gnostic possibilities from there. However, the proto-orthodox position would appear to be the exact opposite of the Valentinian Gnosticism mentioned in the last chapter, where Christ was neither God nor man.

Interestingly, there was a twentieth-century movement that embraced the dominant tenets of all three of the proto-orthodox competitors. The Positive Christianity Movement (1933–1945), promoted by Adolf Hitler and the Nazi Party, rejected the belief that Christ was God—in agreement with the Ebionites. Additionally, for obvious reasons, they also rejected everything Jewish, including the Old Testament, just like the Marcionites. Finally, like the Gnostics, Hitler believed that he had secret knowledge and a secret connection to the divine that he called *Providence*. As evidence of his personal supernatural connection, he cited his miraculous escapes from no less than fourteen assassination attempts from 1933 through 1945, as well as his survival of the 1923 Beer Hall Putsch. In that 1923 protest, the man with whom he had linked arms was shot dead by police; Hitler suffered only a shoulder injury while being dragged to the ground by the dying man. On July, 20, 1944, Claus von Stauffenberg famously placed a powerful bomb at Hitler's feet during a staff meeting. While the blast killed four and injured thirteen, a mind-boggling series of coincidences (e.g., time of meeting moved up, meeting place moved from solid enclosed bunker to room with windows, second bomb left out of briefcase, bomb moved away from his feet, heavy wooden table between him and the blast, while at detonation he just happened to be leaning all the way over to point to a map position in the middle of the table, etc.) resulted in Hitler's own injuries being so superficial that he was able to keep his appointment to greet Mussolini at the local railway station later that very same afternoon. There is absolutely no doubt about the extraordinary nature of his otherworldly chain of escapes, which *der Fuhrer* himself attributed to divine intervention. However, while his subordinates could not deny this uncanny string of apparently supernatural happenstances, they were a little more realistic in their assessment of the source of his spiritual connection. They concluded: "Hitler has a guardian Devil."[1] Similarly, Christian martyr Dietrich Bonhoeffer in *The Cost of Discipleship*

---

1. Moorhouse, *Killing Hitler*, 248.

wrote that Hitler "was the Antichrist."[2] Equivalent sentiments were probably shared by the relatively small number of unflinching Lutheran and Catholic Church members who refused to go along with the hysterical masses in idolizing Germany's new god; they quietly clung to their prewar foundational beliefs, and, most importantly, their worship of Christ as God.

In the first centuries of Christianity, it was not at all clear as to whether Christ was man, God, neither, or both. Few today can even believe that these diverse theologies were viable teachings at the time and that all were spreading rapidly. Because proto-orthodoxy has been the standard for nearly two millennia, even secular people might find it hard to believe that early Christians were readily embracing divine aeons, male-female Godheads, and Christs; a Jesus who was on the cross and a Christ who wasn't; and an evil creator demiurge, as well as the medley of other beliefs mentioned in the prior chapters. Formulating a uniform theology was a luxury not afforded to dispersed, fledgling, underground, often persecuted communities.

Tertullian's statement that the blood of the martyrs is the seed of the church had been proven accurate during the first 300 years of intermittent persecutions of the Christian community. It is estimated that during the 249 years between Nero and Constantine, 129 of those years were marked by state-sponsored persecution, while during 120 of those years Christians were tolerated by imperial authority.[3] However, that neat divide clouds the reality that during the entire 249 years, Christians were subject to local persecutions throughout the empire. Christians were easy targets since there was no distinction between religion and politics. The emperor was both head of state and head of the Roman state religion. On top of this, superstition abounded throughout the empire. If there were some local catastrophe, people might conclude that the pagan gods had been angered by this rebellious Christian sect refusing to give them their due. Moreover, since the Christians were to blame, retribution and punishment would be seen

2. Bonhoeffer, *Cost of Discipleship*, 29.
3. Boer, *St. Ignatius of Antioch*, 34.

as an appropriate course of action. This was the mentality of the time. The same mentality is seen in the Old Testament book of Jeremiah (44:15–18), where it was said that some Jews were attributing their woes to offenses against the pagan gods. They told Jeremiah that they would not listen to him, because "ever since we stopped burning incense to the Queen of Heaven and pouring out drink offerings to her, we have had nothing and have been perishing by the sword and famine." Jumping ahead to the 400s, St. Augustine wrote *The City of God* to counter the claim by pagan Romans that the successful Germanic invasions were punishment from the pagan gods for the empire casting them aside and embracing Christianity.

However, it's not as if Roman society was comprised of a bunch of religious zealots. The Roman Empire was pretty much "live and let live" and tolerated a wide variety of beliefs in its vast realm of some sixty million people. The sticking point for the Christians was their insistence on exclusivity. Rome allowed diverse practices and beliefs but demanded at least a token of appreciation for demigod emperors and the traditional Roman religion in the interest of empire-wide unity. As Paul Boer explains, "Acceptance of the national religion in antiquity was an obligation incumbent upon all citizens; failure to worship the gods of the state was equivalent to treason."[4] Devout Christians refused to play along, even in regard to a simple token sacrifice to the emperor or the Roman gods. Interestingly, the Jews had much the same exclusive mindset but were allowed to remain distinct because of the Romans' respect for the antiquity of their religion. As soon as there was a clear distinction between Judaism and this new Christian sect, it was generally open season on local Christians throughout the empire until the reign of Constantine.

Regardless of what a person actually believed, simply being labeled a Christian was enough to endanger your life and your health. One of the writings of the man who was bishop of Carthage, Saint Cyprian (c. AD 200–258), might be helpful in giving us some grasp of the theological realities of the early Christian era.

4. Boer, *St. Ignatius of Antioch*, 28.

He denied the appellation *martyr* for those who were murdered by the Romans for calling themselves Christians, when in actuality they were engaged in the worship of a multiplicity of divine aeons or a phantom. Cyprian realized that the Romans weren't exactly splitting hairs and carefully differentiating between factions and were therefore murdering Christians from all of the prevalent groups (and even other groups not mentioned). In light of this, he wrote that one "cannot be a martyr who is not in the Church."[5] In other words, Cyprian was soberly stating that some of those being crucified, fed to the lions, tortured to death, and otherwise brutalized were outside of Christianity and therefore not to be classified as Christian martyrs. They may have been sincere and supremely committed to their beliefs, but, according to Cyprian, the beliefs they were dying for were not Christian.

One of those who did suffer a famous martyrdom for the correct (proto-orthodox) Christian beliefs was another disciple of the apostle John, Ignatius of Antioch (c. AD 35–108), who would ultimately die on the grand stage of the empire. Antioch, the so-called cradle of Christianity, where Ignatius was appointed bishop by Peter, was a long way from Rome. However, like the apostle Paul decades earlier, he, too, was transported to Rome to be judged by the emperor. After a long trip where he wrote several letters and met personally with other famous proto-orthodox leaders, he was ultimately torn apart by lions in the Roman Colosseum on the orders of Emperor Trajan around AD 108.

We are familiar with Ignatius and several other prominent proto-orthodox patriarchs due to their famous deaths, enduring statements, and/or because some modern-day churches have been named in honor of them. St. Polycarp is familiar to many today because of his martyrdom, famous last words, and—most importantly—his tutelage under the beloved disciple. It is common knowledge that Polycarp (born between AD 60 and 69) was a disciple of the apostle and Gospel writer John. Tertullian, Jerome, and others tell us that he had been appointed by John to be the bishop of Smyrna, which was the second of the seven churches to

5. Boer, *St. Ignatius of Antioch*, 26.

receive letters from Christ in the book of Revelation. Other early writers also testify to the veracity of the above statements with Irenaeus, poignantly adding that Polycarp "was not only instructed by Apostles, [but] had been the companion of many that had seen Christ"; he goes on to say that Polycarp "constantly taught what he had learned from the Apostles." Then in another letter (to Victor), Irenaeus tells of Polycarp's trip to Rome and some minor discrepancy he had with the Roman church leader named Anicetus, whom he says "was unable to persuade Polycarp not to observe the customs he had always observed with John, the Lord's disciple, and with the rest of the Apostles in whose company he had lived."[6]

Thus, in Polycarp we have a man who was the disciple of John, was appointed by him to lead the Church of Smyrna, was also instructed by the other apostles, knew them personally, and even lived with the apostles who had been with Christ. Needless to say, if one is looking for the true meaning of John's Gospel and exactly what the New Testament writers believed about Christ, Polycarp's understandings are about as close to the fountainhead as one can get. Although a great deal is known about his martyrdom, little is known about Polycarp's early life, and, unfortunately, his only surviving complete manuscript is his letter to the Philippians. We are, however, fortunate to have a very detailed compilation of his beliefs from his disciple, Irenaeus. Converted from paganism at age sixteen by Polycarp, Irenaeus studied with him for the next ten years. In a letter to Papias, bishop of Hierapolis, Irenaeus writes:

> When I was still a boy, I saw thee in Lower Asia [when Polycarp distinguished himself] splendidly in the imperial court and [you were boldly standing] with him. For I remember the events of that time more clearly than what is of recent occurrence. The lessons learned in childhood [age sixteen to twenty-six] grow with the growth of the soul, and become one with it; and so, I am able to tell even the spot where the blessed Polycarp used to sit and discourse, his goings out and his comings in, his manner of life, his personal appearance, and the public

6. Jackson, *Early Church Classics*, 9–10.

> discourses which he used to give. I remember how he used to tell of his [interactions] with John, and with the rest of those who had seen the Lord, and how he recalled and related their words. And such particulars as he had heard concerning the Lord, and concerning His mighty works, and concerning His teaching, Polycarp, as having derived them from the eye-witnesses of the life of the Word, used to tell without exception in harmony with the Scriptures. To these things by God's mercy I used to listen with all my might, noting them down from time to time, if not on paper, in my heart; and ever by God's grace I faithfully turn them over and over in my mind.[7]

We will see later how close Polycarp and his disciple Irenaeus actually were and how carefully the latter must have listened in order to debunk many heresies of the time with uncommon boldness, profound insight, and incredible depth. Much of Polycarp's life is known only because Irenaeus relayed many "accounts, descriptions, and even conversations Polycarp had held with John."[8]

In his martyrdom, which unlike his life we know much about, Polycarp would not denounce Christ and famously stated to the Roman proconsul inside the arena at Smyrna, "Eighty and six years have I served him, and he never did me any injury: how can I blaspheme my King and my Savior?"[9] Since he was well aware that other Christians had been brutally murdered in the arena before he had arrived, the proconsul threatened to call in the wild beasts in an effort to frighten him into repentance. Polycarp replied, "Call them then, for we are not accustomed to repent of what is good in order to adopt that which is evil."[10] In the end, a Roman soldier killed Polycarp with one thrust of his spear.

Polycarp's surviving letter to the Philippians, being more focused on exhortation and instruction, does not directly address the issue of who Christ is. However, several of his statements unequivocally define his position. In chapter 2, referring to Christ,

7. Jackson, *Early Church Classics*, 11–12.

8. Polycarp, *Sacred Writings*, 1–2.

9. Polycarp, *Sacred Writings*, 13.

10. Polycarp, *Sacred Writings*, 14.

he says, "To Him all things in heaven and on earth are subject. Him every spirit serves."[11] Almost two centuries later, the Eastern Church patriarch Gregory of Nazianzus makes the issue of who you serve one of his most important christological arguments when he writes: "If I worshipped a creature [created being], I would not be called a Christian. Why is Christianity precious? Is it not that Christ is God?"[12]

Again, in chapters 5 and 6 of his letter to the Philippians, Polycarp makes similar statements about serving Christ. First, he says, "In like manner should the deacons be blameless before the face of His righteousness, as being the servants of God and Christ."[13] Then, after quoting 2 Cor 5:10 in the translation he was using ("We must all appear at the judgment-seat of Christ and must every one give an account of himself"), he elaborates and, speaking of Christ, says: "Let us then serve Him in fear, and with all reverence, as He himself commanded us, and as the apostles preached the Gospel unto us."[14] Certainly Rom 1:18–25 is unambiguous in declaring that the godless and the wicked worship and serve the creature rather than the Creator. Even those groups that do not believe in the divinity of Christ try to obfuscate those verses where Christ is said to be worshiped by substituting "did obeisance" to Christ (New World Translation). By doing so, they, too, appear to recognize the significance of serving and worshipping anyone but God. Certainly, those who endured agonizingly torturous deaths for their insistence on the worship of Christ and their steadfast refusal to offer even token worship to the emperor understood the significance of the issue. To them, it was a matter of eternal life and bodily death on one hand, or bodily life and eternal death on the other. The two positions were mutually exclusive; and those we remember to this day, like most of the apostles, chose the former.

Unfortunately, after the death of the original apostles and those who knew them, such as Polycarp, the church was faced

11. Polycarp, *Sacred Writings*, 3.

12. Beeley, *Gregory of Nazianzus*, 125.

13. Polycarp, *Sacred Writings*, 4.

14. Polycarp, *Sacred Writings*, 5.

with even greater challenges than the Roman opposition. There is almost unanimous historical agreement that Christianity as taught by Jesus faced an existential threat that nearly engulfed the entire movement. Throughout the late first and entire second centuries, the Gnostics, with their scriptural counterfeits and secret knowledge, as well as the Marcionites, with their edited writings and charismatic founder, were actively spreading their various ideas and systems all over the empire (as stated in the first two chapters). The Christianity that had been taught by the apostles was under siege, and many of the proto-orthodox were alarmed.

Before they were martyred, both Polycarp of Smyrna and Ignatius of Antioch recognized the threat posed by the plethora of false teachings being spread around the Mediterranean world in the early second century. Ignatius was one of the first to call for structure and uniformity in the church in the form of local bishops who not only would have the final word in each city but also would meet with bishops from other cities to settle more complicated issues. The first-century letters of Paul show that deviant teachings arose almost immediately after he departed from many of the churches he founded. The same pattern is clearly evident in the book of Revelation, where Christ addresses a variety of diverse teachings in the seven letters to the seven churches. The fact that the seven churches were in relatively close proximity to one another should have made their differences minimal, but obviously it didn't. Consequently, it's hardly surprising that teachings in geographically distant locales, such as the Eastern Empire, the Western Empire, North Africa, and beyond, were even more diverse than noted in the earlier chapters. In addition to the three groups mentioned, outright blasphemous distortions were being vigorously distributed by groups led by people such as Ptolemaeus, Ptolemy, Colorbasus, Marcus, Carprocrates, and Cerinthus, and groups such as the Barbeliotes, the Cainites—and many, many others. All of these conflicting groups were rushing in to fill the void left by the original apostles and their immediate successors, and it's likely that had they all continued to grow, flourish and splinter, Christianity in our own day and age would not be recognizable. By the end of the second century, theological fragmentation, outright apostasy, and spreading heresy threatened the annihilation of any semblance of Christ's message.

There was no structure in place to keep everyone in check and, as a result, theological anarchy reigned. Although we intermittently read about the "catholic" church in many early writings, it was not the large-c Catholic Church organization that we are all familiar with today. *Catholic* was simply a word that meant universal. So rather than some governing organization, the name referred to every true Christian who was considered part of the "catholic/universal" church. It's in the letter to Smyrna written by Ignatius that

> we first find the use of the phrase catholic church in patristic writings. He defines it as to be found "where Jesus Christ is," words which certainly do not limit it to communication with the professed successor to Saint Peter. [In fact, his] Epistle to the Romans is totally inconsistent with any conception on his part, that Rome was the see and residence of a bishop holding any other than fraternal relations with himself.[15]

In the Nicene Creed, in the words "I believe in one, holy, catholic and apostolic Church," the use of "catholic" has absolutely nothing to do with the later Roman Catholic Church. The Greek writers were stating that they believed in a "universal" church found any place where Jesus Christ is. Anyone writing that the two are synonymous because both are designated by the term *catholic* (and there are many) would be scholastically equivalent to someone writing that the billion plus people in the South Asian nation of India are synonymous with the Mohawk, Iroquois, Apache, and the like because both are designated by the term *Indian*.

It is also noteworthy that, beginning with Nicaea, the first four ecumenical councils (ecumenical being Greek for "from the whole world," held in 325, 381, 431, and 451), were all in the East, all conducted in Greek, and were not attended by any pope. These are the four councils that produced the creeds and christological

15. Boer, *St. Ignatius of Antioch*, 43.

essentials that went on to define Christianity for the next 1600 years and down through today. Without any governing structure, how was this all sorted out, cleaned up, and organized in such a way that the original message of Jesus has been preserved for us almost two thousand years later? Most today are not even aware that Christianity was ever at these crossroads and that it was somehow able to tunnel through this virtual mountain of heresies and distorted writings and come out the other side. Who did the digging?

As the documentary *Ancient Roads from Christ to Constantine* eloquently states regarding the situation faced in the aftermath of the death of the apostles and those they taught, "The battle for Christianity was entering the next phase and the leader of this fight was a man who lived in Gaul. . . . This man would exert a crucial role in defining early Christianity."[16] Various sources speak about this same man, saying that he was a "cleric noted for his role in guiding and expanding Christian communities in what is now the south of France and, more widely, for the development of Christian theology by combating heresy and defining orthodoxy."[17] Most importantly for all of us today is that he classified as Scripture not only the Old Testament but most books now known as the New Testament,[18] while excluding many works, a large number by Gnostics, that flourished in the second century and claimed scriptural authority.[19]

Before him, Christians differed as to which Gospel they preferred.[20] He asserted that the four Gospels, Matthew, Mark, Luke, John, were canonical Scripture, thus providing the earliest witness to the assertion of the four canonical Gospels.[21]

Every Christian denomination today, whether any form of Protestantism, Catholicism, Eastern Orthodoxy, or even some

16. Phillips, "From Apocalypse To Heresies," in *Ancient Roads*, disc 2, lect. 1, 1:00.

17. Poncelet, "St. Irenaeus."

18. Cross, *Oxford Dictionary of Christian Church*.

19. Wingren, "St. Irenaeus."

20. Harris, *Understanding the Bible*, cited in "Irenaeus."

21. Irenaeus, *Against Heresies*, bk 3, 428.

that are considered cults, owe some gratitude to this one man, his canon of Scripture, and his leading role in combating heresy and defining orthodoxy. And that one man was the aforementioned disciple of Polycarp, Irenaeus, who, after leaving his home town of Smyrna, journeyed some 1700 miles and ended up settling in and becoming bishop of what is now Lyon, France. The irony of the battle for Christianity being fought 2700 miles from Jerusalem, 2600 miles from Antioch, and over 600 miles from Rome is not lost on historians.

In the last chapter of this book, some of the definitive writings of Irenaeus in regard to the nature of Christ will be explored. We are fortunate that his seminal five-volume book, *Against Heresies*, still exists today. However, before his writings could be distributed, appreciated, and ultimately lead to the ushering in of an empire-wide assimilation of apostle John's/Polycarp's Christology, the political atmosphere had to change and the persecutions had to end. That will be the focus of the next chapter.

4

The Persecution's End

IRENAEUS DIED AROUND 202 BC, and it would be more than a hundred years before Christians would be able to worship without being targeted or persecuted. During that third century, writers such as Cyprian, Clement of Alexandria, Tertullian, Hippolytus, Dionysius, Origen, Gregory Thaumaturgus (Gregory the Miracle-Worker), and many, many others fought for their interpretations and values and contributed greatly to Christianity. Even dissenting ideas were highly valuable because they forced both foe and friend alike to solidify the salient points of their positions and to pray for guidance a little more earnestly. Although many more volumes than those already in existence could be written about these men, they all shared the misfortune of writing at a time when free Christian expression was severely hindered by the Roman Empire and also before the Christian canon had been solidified. Correspondingly, it was not an ideal environment for reciprocal theological debate; more importantly, it was not conducive to the fomenting of a uniform theology about the nature of Christ, which is the primary focus of this book. As alluded to earlier, the finer points of any theology cannot be adequately sorted out while the adherents are using different scriptural books—isolated from one another, underground, and often running for their lives.

Following one of the worst of the empire-wide persecutions during the reign of Diocletian (emperor AD 284–305), the era of toleration began with the reign of Constantine (emperor AD 306–337). The Edict of Milan in AD 313 proclaimed that everyone in the empire could now worship freely in whatever way they desired. Additionally, Christians were granted specific liberties, given a favored status, and in many cases even had their confiscated property returned to them. One of the more obvious perks of their new favored status was that the state officially sponsored the building of churches and then proceeded to declare them tax exempt. However, contrary to widespread erroneous reporting, Constantine did not make Christianity the official religion of the Roman Empire. That did not happen until the reign of Emperor Theodosius the First, almost seventy years later. Finally, Christians could openly debate, communicate, assemble, and worship. Most significantly, they were now free to travel all over the empire for the purpose of congregating in one location to examine, and thereby attempt to resolve, divisive theological issues. However, in spite of the end to individual Christians being crucified, tortured, set on fire, fed to the lions, and worse, there was a downside that exists with us to this very day. All of Christianity being accepted and tolerated was beneficial; however, all of Christianity actually earning favored status within the empire was fraught with unforeseen negative consequences.

It is estimated that during the persecutions, no more than 10 percent of the empire-wide population was made up of all of the groups previously mentioned who were claiming to be Christian. What they lacked in numbers, they made up for in commitment. Being a Christian was a very dangerous profession during the era of persecutions; therefore, the overwhelming percentage of those claiming to be such were deeply devoted to their beliefs. Few were inclined to pretend to be something they were not when the cost of this pointless charade might be death. So, during that time what you truly had was a *community of saints*. In spite of the term being loosely tossed around today, the early Christians were infinitely closer to the ideal because there was no doubt that they were laying everything on the line for their beliefs. Everything they had and everything they were could be taken from them at any moment because they openly and exclusively confessed complete devotion to Christ. It wasn't just their property and their lives (although that would seem to be concern-worthy enough). On top of death itself, there was the unique, well-thought-out methodology and message-sending process that awaited them. They were all aware that the Romans prided themselves on carrying out torturous, painful, public executions and over-the-top, blood-filled entertainment events in order to discourage dissention.

Depending on one's perspective, there may have been a fate even worse than death, as Paul Boer contends:

> Almost worse than all this was the penal servitude to which bishops, priests, deacons, laymen and women, and even children, were condemned in some of the more violent persecutions; these refined personages of both sexes, victims of merciless laws were doomed to pass the remainder of their days in the darkness of the mines, where they dragged out a wretched existence, half naked, hungry and with no bed save the damp ground. Those were far more fortunate who were condemned to even the most disgraceful death, in the arena, or by crucifixion.[1]

After Christianity became the favored religion of the state, all types of people, with varying levels of commitment, jumped on the bandwagon because Christianity suddenly presented an opportunity for them to benefit themselves. Soon, the percentage of Christians in the empire quickly ballooned to some 50 percent of the population. So, while the number of Christians dramatically rose after the decrees of Constantine, the percentage of those who were noncommitted, lukewarm, nominal Christians also rose dramatically. In effect, you now had a lot more Christians who, ironically, were a lot less Christian. One's motivation for becoming Christian also came into question. Paraphrasing Ronald Herzman of State University of New York (SUNY), before Constantine, if

1. Boer, *St. Ignatius of Antioch*, 39.

someone admitted to the local census taker that he was a Christian, he might be invited to dinner—at the five o'clock feeding of the lions. After Constantine, the same admission might result in an appointment to a desirable job. The emperor was now looking for some "good Christian folk" to fill a slew of highly desirable and lucrative positions.[2]

Lest you think Ronald Herzman's statement is an exaggeration, Justin Martyr recounts an episode where the simple accusation by an angry husband led to four hasty executions, including the prime target of his vindictiveness, his wife:

> A woman who had been converted to Christianity was accused by her husband before the magistrate of being Christian. . . . [In addition to the woman,] her angry husband caused the arrest of the [missionary who converted her, who], when questioned, acknowledged that he was a Christian and was condemned to death. In the court, at the time this sentence was pronounced, were two persons who protested against the inequity of inflicting capital punishment for the mere fact of professing Christianity. The magistrate in reply asked if they were also Christians, and on their answering in the affirmative both were ordered to be executed. [All this] on the accusation of a man actuated by malice, solely for the reason that his wife had given up the evil life she had previously led in his society.[3]

Thus, Christianity went from a small group, distinct from the general population and wholeheartedly devoted to God, to a large group, living pretty much as the general population lived and possibly devoted only to self—from missionaries to mercenaries. The majority of life-and-death propositions leave only two dichotomous options, with no middle ground. During the persecution era, one either invested oneself entirely in one's particular form of Christianity or didn't bother with Christianity at all. However, toleration opened up a multiplicity of options and entry-level

2. Cook and Herzman, "Augustine and the World of Classical Antiquity," in *St. Augustine's* Confessions, disc 1, lect. 2, 24:30.

3. Justin Martyr, quoted in Boer, *St. Ignatius of Antioch*, 34–35.

investment tiers, including the prevalent one-foot-here-and-one-foot-there, hedge-betting investiture in vogue throughout most of Christian history. In a short span, the adherents went from a community of committed Christians to a community of involved Christians. The old explanation regarding the difference between the two positions is applicable here: "If you had bacon and eggs this morning for breakfast, the animal that gave the eggs was involved, while the animal that gave the bacon was committed."

In any event, at the beginning of the fourth century, the last major persecution under Diocletian ended and, shortly thereafter, the era of toleration under Emperor Constantine began. The conception that Constantine came into power, dictated the proto-orthodox position that Christ was God, and settled the matter could hardly be further from the truth. It wasn't even settled after it was supposed to have been settled, because Constantine, regardless of whether he was genuine in his conversion or not, was hardly a theologian. He was a politician who convened the Council of Nicaea, first and foremost, in the interest of empire-wide theological unity.

With the new religious freedoms an interesting dilemma arose. There were a fickle, feckless minority, even during the persecutions, who gave up their Christianity when the cost was too high and then tried to come back to the church when things were safer. The group that refused to allow them to reenter fellowship, following the time of persecution, became known as the Donatists (yet another sect). Thus ensued what became known as the Donatist controversy. In a nutshell, the religious leaders who returned to the church and wanted their old authority and positions back were opposed by the Donatists, who said that they had forfeited everything when they turned tail and ran. The real sticking point was the insistence by the Donatists that everything that these elders had done in service to the people and to the church should be invalidated. This meant, for example, that if this elder had performed the marriage ceremony for you and your wife, you were not really married because he was an "imposter" (according to the Donatists) at the time he performed your union; therefore, your children were illegitimate. The Donatists took their stance even further by insisting that elders must be relatively faultless in their personal lives, and if not, their service should likewise be invalidated. That meant, for example, that if someone had been an elder for forty years and had not fled the persecution but was discovered at the end of that time to have had a long-term mistress, then everything he officiated over was null and void. Calmer minds prevailed; the chaos that this view would have created was extrapolated and recognized; and it was ultimately decided that the office still maintained its authority, regardless of the behavior of the officeholder. Of course, that is pretty much the way things remain today. If a Catholic priest or Protestant minister is found to be less than honorable, the secretary from the church they represent doesn't get on the phone and call the people they married or baptized over the last thirty years and say, "Guess what?" No, the actions of the office are still valid in spite of the immoral actions of the officeholder.

At the opposite end of the spectrum from the rigid Donatists were a minority of wealthy Christians, who engaged in shenanigans for the purpose of skirting the law in a manner endemic to all generations. They were able to play both ends against the middle and thereby not deny Christ, while at the same time keep themselves from being executed. A simple bribe to the magistrate procured for them a genuine certificate of compliance, and the matter was settled neatly and expeditiously—with the emperor, and presumably Christ, being none the wiser.

As evidenced in earlier chapters, Christianities, oftentimes with very little discernible connection, abounded throughout the empire. Previous emperors had persecuted the Christians, not on theological grounds, as they neither cared about nor understood such issues, but rather on the basis of empire-wide unity. This was also Constantine's primary motivation in trying to uniformly define a singular, recognizable form of Christianity. Emperors who followed him on the throne and were not proto-orthodox would later try to legislate their own Christology, again only in the interest of unity. Ultimately, and as we shall see only temporarily, the Council of Nicaea in AD 325 did conclude that Scripture teaches the full divinity of Christ (as impossible as that concept is to comprehend). However, Emperor Constantine himself had little understanding of theological issues that were debated before him, as evidenced by the fact that shortly before his death in AD 337, he was baptized by an Arian bishop. Arius believed that Jesus was a created being, and, therefore, Arius was on the losing end of the scriptural debate at Nicaea. Why would an emperor who had just presided over a council that declared Arianism a heresy allow himself to be baptized by an Arian bishop? Baptism was particularly important during that time because the powerful (and even laypeople) waited until the very end of their lives before having all their sins expunged by baptism. They calculated that they could continue to blatantly sin right up until the last minute of their lives. It was personally imperative that Constantine did this right because he had ordered the execution of his son and then followed that deed by facilitating the merciless drowning of his wife in an overheated bath. Would he have taken the chance that those two heinous acts might not be erased had he fully understood that the man authorized by God to erase those sins was a heretic and therefore was most probably not authorized by God? Not only was he baptized by a bishop embracing what the council that he convened had concluded was heresy, but also, he had prearranged for another Arian bishop to deliver his eulogy after his death!

Following Constantine's death, the debate about the nature of Christ continued unabated. All of Christianity is fortunate that the debate took place in the East because Greek is so much more exacting a language than most of the world's tongues, with many different words expressing different ideas or degrees of a concept that in English might be represented by only one word. Moreover, because Greek is the language in which the New Testament was written, these Eastern theologians had more insight and understanding of the original meanings than we obtain from our translations today. Some of the issues argued over today were not even on the table back then because the Greek-speaking world understood exactly what the Greek-speaking New Testament writers were saying, and our English translation may imply something else. For example, in his letter to the Philippians, Polycarp wrote that whoever perverts the Gospels "and says that there is neither a resurrection nor judgment, he is the firstborn of Satan."[4] In *Against Heresies*, Irenaeus recounts the meeting between Polycarp and Marcion in Rome, where Polycarp says to Marcion, "I do know thee, the firstborn of Satan."[5] Either Irenaeus, who quoted this, and Polycarp, the disciple of the apostle John (all three being native Greek speakers) were trying to introduce a new doctrine by informing us that "the first thing that the co-creator Satan created was Marcion," or they were telling us that the word "firstborn" is commonly used among them to signify "preeminent." Therefore, they were saying that "Marcion is preeminent among the evil." Obviously, the interpretation that Satan is a co-creator is patently absurd. Furthermore, the initial quote says that any person at any time who rejects the resurrection and judgment "is the firstborn of Satan." So, inarguably, Polycarp is saying that all of the people who reject those two doctrines, whether this year, next year, or the year after that—every one of them is "preeminent among the evil." Therefore, Jesus being called "the firstborn of the dead" and "the firstborn over all creation" in King James English does not at all imply in Greek that he was the first thing that God created, just as "the firstborn of Satan" in Greek does not imply that Marcion was the first thing that Satan created. Some modern organizations try to use the English translation "firstborn" as one of the proofs for their "created Christ" theology. Consistent with Irenaeus and Polycarp, the meaning plainly appears to be "preeminent over all creation" and "preeminent over the resurrected."

The above also points out the necessity of investigating all new ideas and theologies with exhaustive scholarship rather than superficial scholarship. While it is not impossible that someone may discover a scriptural nugget that has been overlooked for two thousand years, it is unlikely. But even if the nugget is there waiting to be plucked, no one can build error-free theologies around words in other languages without knowing the indigenous meaning

4. Polycarp, *Sacred Writings*, 5.

5. Irenaeus, *Against Heresies*, bk 3, 416.

of those foreign words. Anyone putting forth a new theological system must unequivocally ensure that their biblical reasoning is airtight and bulletproof. If it truly is, then they may indeed have found something new and improved. However, the overwhelming odds are that they are just recycling a heresy that was adequately and definitively refuted in the past. This is especially true today in light of at least nine warnings in Matt 24 about deception as the number one sign of the end of times. This applies not only to perceived cults but also to everyone, since many new ideas and freedoms that would be totally alien to Christians of the last 1600 years have become mainstream teachings today. Have we changed Christianity in our day in order to conform to the realities of the way that modern people prefer to live instead of allowing Christianity to change the way we live? In many quarters it seems that there have been very substantial changes, even in the short period of our own lifetimes. All modern Christians might wish to ponder what Polycarp wrote about the Christians living toward the end of his life, many of whom were being martyred, in comparison to the Christians alive at the beginning of his life who also accompanied the apostles. He wrote: "I am humbled and abashed in comparing what a Christian used to be, with what a Christian is, in our times, even at his best estate."[6] That statement is provocative in any language and in any epoch, and even today, since what a Christian used to be even seventy years ago is a far cry from what a Christian is in our times.

Reasoning and debating in the same language in which the New Testament was written constituted a great advantage in trying to understand the true nature of Christ. It is already a difficult and deep subject, so just imagine the confusion that these ancient theologians would have had if the apostles had written in Chinese and the early patriarchs were working with a Greek translation. However, thankfully, it was both written and sorted out by native Greek speakers. All sides of this debate in the fourth century realized that in Jesus Christ, something brand new and almost inconceivable had come into the world. As stated by Christopher Beeley,

6. Polycarp, *Sacred Writings*, 8.

"even the most extreme anti-Nicene theologians in the fourth century—such as Arius, Aetius, and Eunomius—all believe that the Son of God, who is in some sense divine, became flesh for the salvation of the human race."[7]

It is noteworthy that Arius and others had their shot at being endorsed by an emperor after the Council of Nicaea. Following the death of Constantine in AD 337, his three sons divided the empire. In the West, Constantine II and his younger brother Constans were quickly at each other's throats and soon consumed by their competing ambitions. In the East, Constantius II, a believer in Arian theology, sought to enforce Arianism over the areas that are now Turkey, Syria, Israel, and northern Egypt. In a fitting imitation of his father, in AD 357 he convened the Council of Sirmium, which ultimately refuted the conclusion from the Council of Nicaea in favor of Homoianism. In contrast to the Nicene Creed, which said that Christ and the Father are made of the same substance and equal, Homoianism declared that Christ was like the Father. To make it all official, Constantius II commissioned the Dated Creed in AD 359 that prohibited any Nicene language and insisted on Homoian Christianity. Also, in the AD 350s, there arose another group that attempted to downgrade Christ's status even further. These were the Heterousians, who said that Christ was unlike the Father in essence (which is what their name means).

After the death of Constantius II in AD 361, all sides were thrown a curve when Julian the Apostate became the last Roman pagan emperor. He was opposed to Christianity altogether and sought to restore the good old days of the ancient pagan cults. The tables turned again in AD 363, when Julian suddenly died and was succeeded by the Nicene Emperor Jovian. Unfortunately for the proto-orthodox, Jovian reigned for only a year and was succeeded by the Homoian Emperor Valens, whose lengthy fourteen-year reign, from AD 364 to378, had a substantial impact on Christianity. It was during this time that many prominent proto-orthodox were persecuted, arrested, or exiled, and Homoian Christology was again the official doctrine of the Eastern Empire. However, in

7. Beeley, *Gregory of Nazianzus*, 124.

AD 378, Emperor Valens was killed in battle and was replaced by the pro-Nicene Emperor Theodosius in AD 379. Theodosius the Great reigned from AD 379 through 395 and was the last emperor to rule over both the Eastern and the Western halves of the Roman Empire.

The last two paragraphs cover a lot of ground, and many volumes could and have been written about the events and rulers of that time. For our purposes, what is most germane is the fact that the widespread Christian debate that began with Constantine never fully returned to the old oppressive second-century pattern. Highly divergent teachings such as Gnosticism and Marcionism could not continue their remarkable growth in the penetrating light of widespread, fundamentally scriptural, back-and-forth debate. The far-flung theologies that easily took root in the hands of charismatic leaders could not survive in this more heliocentric atmosphere. From all quarters the debate was now focused squarely on the Son.

The Eastern Orthodox patriarch Gregory of Nazianzus (posthumously awarded the title, Gregory the Theologian, in AD 451) was widely regarded as the greatest theologian of the fourth century. He had labeled all these continually changing christological theologies, which were motivated by the whims of whoever happened to be the emperor at the time, "Christ-trading," and in one out-of-character sarcastic sermon, he issued an "invitation for people to step right up and change their views again, since variety is the spice of life."[8] Author Christopher Beeley confirms what was stated a few paragraphs earlier about the ruling at Nicaea some three decades earlier, hardly settling the matter: "When Gregory began his ecclesiastical career in the early 360s, the Trinitarian faith of his upbringing was out of step with the official imperial doctrine. Since his ascension as sole emperor in 351, Constantius II had aggressively promoted the ecclesiastical unity of the empire on the basis of a particular, narrow-minded version of the old Eusebian [Homoian] theology."[9] Gregory himself underlines

8. Beeley, *Gregory of Nazianzus*, 49.

9. Beeley, *Gregory of Nazianzus*, 17.

the chronic factionalism in Christianity as late as AD 379, when he speaks about "so many Pauls, Apolloses, and Cephases, and so many Christs."[10]

Gregory also speaks temperately about a major problem that many proto-orthodox writers noted: namely, how to go about conveying the deep and complicated issue of Christ's divinity to an empire-wide population where roughly 90 percent of the people could not read or write. Gregory encourages the simple to "leave sophisticated language to the more advanced."[11] This was probably sound advice in a society where the illiteracy rate was astronomical and only the wealthy were educated. Consequently, the simplistic, easily understood appeal of a "created Christ" was the most easily digestible concept for these uneducated masses; therefore, the most uncomplicated postulations were the ones that were readily embraced by the 90 percent illiterate population. The same problem would arise later when the Germanic tribes overran the empire. A great many of these tribes took illiteracy and backwardness to a new level by not even having a written language or written history. The Arian missionaries of the early years found in the German barbarians a suitable intellect for their "created Christ" brand of Christianity. Complicated, high Christology was so far beyond their aptitude and capacity that many of the Germanic peoples held their Arian beliefs for generations. They could not accept proto-orthodoxy until long after they settled down in their conquered territories, were assimilated by the educated culture, and became literate.

Irenaeus was not quite as gentle as Gregory in speaking about the illiteracy problem. He wrote that the Marcionites and the Gnostics "cunningly allure the simple-minded to inquire into their system . . . and the simple ones are unable . . . to distinguish falsehood from truth."[12] In speaking of the divinity of Christ, he

10. Beeley, *Gregory of Nazianzus*, 36.

11. Beeley, *Gregory of Nazianzus*, 189.

12. Irenaeus, *Against Heresies*, bk 1, 315.

said that these "profound mysteries . . . do not fall within the range of every intellect."[13]

After centuries of infighting, a monumental milestone was reached in AD 367 that put human intellect in its proper place. The canon proposed by Athanasius, which as mentioned previously is the canon we have today, came to be accepted by most factions. This was a game changer because Scripture rather than human logic became the measuring stick. The arguments of Irenaeus in *Against Heresies*, while scriptural, were completely meaningless to the Gnostics and the Marcionites because they did not accept the books that are part of our canon today. It was like a believer arguing Scripture with an atheist. True, the words might say what the believer says they say, but those words carry no authority or weight with the atheist. It was the same among the Christianities until there was an agreed-upon canon after AD 367. Now something no human could possibly understand could be presented from the point of view of what Scripture stated. Just as with the concept of the eternal existence of God, which is also beyond comprehension, human rationale regarding the nature of Christ now took a back seat to the words of Scripture.

For decades, Gregory of Nazianzus had been emphasizing the inadequacy of human logic. He had written that "God—what he is in nature and being—no human being has ever discovered or can discover . . . we cannot know all of God's infinite essence [because] the deity is not graspable by the human intellect."[14] In regard to his contemporary, the Homoian Eunomius (whom he had debated in person before the Homoian Emperor Valens), Gregory wrote that his real error was claiming "to know God's essence completely."[15] He reiterates that everyone, not just Eunomius, who is absolutely positive about his or her own human rationale in regard to Christ, is in effect claiming to have a complete understanding of God. The offshoot of that concept is the necessity of making the vast and infinite God small enough to fit inside a human head. It can't

13. Irenaeus, *Against Heresies*, bk 1, 315.
14. Beeley, *Gregory of Nazianzus*, 98.
15. Beeley, *Gregory of Nazianzus*, 93.

be done. As Karen Armstrong says in regard to Isa 6:3: "When we use the word 'holy' today, we usually refer to a state of moral excellence. The Hebrew *kaddosh*, however, has nothing to do with morality as such but means 'otherness,' radical separation. . . . The seraphs were crying, Yahweh is other! other! other!"[16] The often expressed thought that a man being able to understand God is like an amoeba being able to understand Einstein is woefully inadequate. God is not a higher form of one of the things we ourselves are; he is "other." Throughout his writings, Gregory hammers away at the issue of God's incomprehensibility time and time again. It must be acknowledged, Gregory insists, that the unlimited, infinite God cannot be fully known or grasped by the limited, finite human mind. Gregory writes that if you, as a human being, refuse to acknowledge the limits of your reason, then sadly, you are "ignorant even of your own ignorance."[17] That admission is the beginning of the necessary humility required to discover the scriptural truth about Christ.

With an agreed-upon canon, some substantive progress was actually made at the Second Ecumenical Council, the Council of Constantinople in AD 381: "Fifty-six years after Nicaea, the Roman Emperor of the East, Theodosius I, convened the second General Council. Because of friction between the emperor who was headquartered in Constantinople and Pope Saint Damasus I, located in Rome, neither the Holy Father nor his papal legates attended. Already the split between East and West was manifesting itself."[18] Again, this was an Eastern Council conducted in the Greek language, with all Eastern bishops. Confirming this, religious historian Richard Kieckhefer states: "This second ecumenical Council, an effort to obtain consensus in the church through an assembly representing all of Christendom, except for the Western church, confirmed the Nicene Creed, expanding the doctrine thereof to produce the Niceno-Constantinopolitan Creed."[19] So, contrary to

16. Armstrong, *History of God*, 41.

17. Beeley, *Gregory of Nazianzus*, 111.

18. Daily Catholic, "Major Councils of Church."

19. Kieckhefer, *Magic in Middle Ages*, 281.

the teaching in some circles that Constantine mandated the Nicene Creed and that the Western Roman popes strong-armed later councils to endorse it, we have seen previously in this chapter and again here that this perception is a fallacy and that the Council of Constantinople represented all of Christendom but excluded the Western church. Since they were still debating in the same Greek language in which the New Testament was written, it is not at all surprising that the Western church (including Rome) was excluded because, as we shall see later, it would be another fifty years before someone presented the case for the divinity of Christ thoroughly and cohesively in the Latin language. Fittingly, all this deep biblical theology was sorted out by native Greek speakers—which is the only way that it could have been done right. Obviously, an already difficult subject will become incomprehensible if compounded by language difficulties. For example, try tackling a difficult subject such as quantum physics using only a Spanish textbook and the language skills you gained in your two years of college Spanish classes. You will not get very far in your understanding. Again, all of Christianity should be grateful that what is often called the most important period in Christian history was sorted out by native Greek speakers.

Finally, with all this "Christ-trading" behind it, Christianity could get down to the business of scripturally defining and cohesively explaining the truth about the nature of Christ. This task fell to a uniquely brilliant, inquisitive, and fastidiously meticulous man, whose writings will be the subject of chapter 6, following a brief, but important, explanation of old and new Arianism in chapter 5.

5

Arianism

Old and New

ARIANISM IS A CATEGORY unto itself that loosely falls somewhere between the Ebionite teachings and one or more of the created Christ Gnostic teachings. Arias was an Alexandrian priest (c. AD 250–336), who taught that the Son of God was created by the Father at some point in time and was therefore neither consubstantial nor coeternal with the Father. Therefore, the most relevant attribute of Arianism is that it denies the full divinity of Jesus Christ. Collaterally, the Homoianism mentioned in the last chapter was one of the many forms of Arianism. And, as with two of the first three groups, original Arian writings have been lost to history. However, we are fortunate that the counterclaims of those who opposed them are so detailed and precise that they provide extensive insight into Arian theology. Just as one can know precisely what a missing wax mold looked like by examining the intricate bronze statue that came out of it, one can know precisely what the Arians believed by examining the negative replica (the intricate rebuttals) that came out of the pens of their detractors. The writings and counterclaims of two of the most meticulous and articulate of those detractors, St. Augustine and Irenaeus, will be covered in detail in chapters 6 and 7. Additionally, Arian theologies have been and continue to be documented because of the creative thinkers who took up this counterfeit cause in the early centuries and because of the many careless readers and sophists who have propagated this heresy throughout Christian history and right on through to the present day.

In spite of the dearth of his original writings, we do know that Arias placed supreme emphasis (as do present-day Arians), on Prov 8:22–25, which says:

> The LORD possessed me in the beginning of his way, before his works of old. I was set up from everlasting, from the beginning, or ever the earth was. When there were no depths, I was brought forth; when there were no fountains abounding with water. Before the mountains were settled, before the hills was I brought forth. (KJV)

Arias believed that the "wisdom" spoken of in the first nine chapters of Proverbs was in reference to Jesus Christ, and therefore, the above verses provided what he believed to be absolute proof that Christ was created or "brought forth." Arias, (as well as present-day careless readers), failed to carefully consider that in those chapters there are at least thirty verses where "wisdom/ Christ" is referred to as a female. Proverbs 7:4 highlights this oversight by declaring, "Say to wisdom, you are my sister." St. Augustine and others will effectively counter this erroneous premise in the following chapter.

Present-day overt Arianism or Semi-Arianism, as exemplified in one form or another by the Jehovah's Witnesses, the Unitarians, and the Mormons, is at least forthright in its presentation. Most in the Christian world believe themselves to be adequately insulated from these blatant Arian influences. They seem to feel that attending their traditional churches, and not opening their doors to proselytizers, puts them beyond the reach of its tentacles. However, insidious covert and cultural Arianism is infecting virtually every Christian church and every individual Christian on the planet. Most are unaware of this epidemic because it does not present itself in the straightforward manner that overt Arianism does. Instead, it is roaming around in disguise under various innocuous sounding subheadings, such as ecumenicalism, humanism, multiculturalism, liberal tolerance, and, of course, modern political correctness. Covert Arianism does not have to come knocking on your door because, unbeknownst to you, it's already in your house. Behind many of the words emanating from TV shows, news reports, movies, newspapers, the internet, and the radio (and even in the commercials), there is some facet of the pluralist agenda. And behind the pluralist agenda is naked covert Arianism.

Lest this sound like the latest, overreaching conspiracy theory, the following quote elucidates the issue perfectly:

> Today Arianism takes a different form, and comes to us in the guise of humanism. By "humanism" I mean that belief system that takes man as the measure of all things. This humanism is a conglomeration of different modernistic beliefs, but the summary of it all is materialism— that this physical world is all there is, human history is all that matters and the advancement of the human race in this physical realm is the only thing [worth] fighting for. Arianism today is an interpretation of Christianity according to this whole materialistic, humanistic philosophy. Clearly, Jesus Christ as the Divine Son of God and the co-eternal second person of the Holy Trinity doesn't really fit. This watered-down Christianity is our modern form of Arianism.[1]

How has the world changed over the last sixty years to effectuate this modern Arianism? Why is "watered-down" Christianity, or casual Christianity, or politically correct Christianity now the norm? Back in 1995 Dennis Okholm and Timothy Phillips were perceptive enough to recognize the embryonic local skirmishes that today, almost twenty-five years later, have devolved into a global conflagration. They wrote that:

> Some theologians are boldly heralding the end of classical Christianity and the beginning of a new millennium in religion. They may not be too far off the mark given the level of political correctness within mainstream churches. Pluralist ideologies, [and] modernity's ethic of civility—which seeks to be tolerant of others—[have]

1. Longenecker, "Arianism Today."

> muted such theologically "offensive" beliefs as God's judgment on sin, the sole authority of Scripture, and salvation through Christ alone. Increasingly, students in Christian colleges are affronted when hearing the traditional claim that salvation is found in Jesus Christ alone.[2]

What has become of the Protestant and Catholic Churches from as near back as the 1960s where the preacher or priest would expound upon sin, and hell, and nonbelievers, and the one way to salvation? How did they morph into these "feel-good churches," with the seventeen-minute sermons that cater to the reported optimum attention span of your average Christian before they tune out? Why, in most cases, have Christian churches become Sunday morning entertainment centers? The answer to these questions is that modern Arianism has happened to them. At its core, modern Arianism rejects the essence of the equality of Jesus Christ with God the Father because it just does not fit well with modern moral sensibilities, modern intellectual rationale, and the pervasive modern scourge of a self-centered, pleasure-filled existence. We may have no issue with the written words or the fundamental doctrines, but how we apply them to our lives, our priorities, and the way we spend our time is a different matter. It would appear that a plethora of "other gods" lord over our lives nowadays and that we ourselves have become "the measure of all things" spiritual. Theology is now subservient to me-ology. And just as the fourth-century Arians become the arbitrators and final editors of Scripture and its practical application, so the modern-day Arians are filling those same shoes.

Those who believe that Jesus Christ is God may fail to see the connection between the loss of the substantive messages of their churches from the 1960s and its replacement with the inconsequential messages of modern Arianism. Hell, sin, the fate of nonbelievers, and salvation through Jesus Christ alone no longer gel with the modern psyche and our modern perception of a "fair God." Our moral and intellectual sensibilities, decimated by continual bombardment from unrelenting waves of humanist assault,

2. Okholm and Phillips, *Four Views on Salvation*, 10–11.

can no longer stand on anything but the softest and most porous theological sand. Almost all of our churches have gone from being built on rock to being built on sand. We will not tolerate moral absolutes. We will not tolerate anything more than empty seventeen-minute sermons interfused with substantial humor and straining to be inoffensive. These sermons are designed, not to build strong Christians, but to address the real present-day priority, which is to ensure that we all come back next week. Can any church really expect to build strong Christians who can resist the pull of the world through seventeen-minute sermons once a week? No. The great majority of churches that used to preach the unvarnished word of Christ either went out of business or decided to conform when their constituents left for the casual Christian churches down the street.

Early Christian dogma is seen as too divisive nowadays, and the exclusivity of Jesus Christ is obviously non-inclusive. It is narrow, rigid, and intolerant. Pluralism, on the other hand, with its "live and let live, let's not judge" and, of course, its sentiment that "other religions may also be salvific" is now almost the obligatory outlook among good, civil, gracious "Christian" people. Particularism is out. But unfortunately, Jesus Christ being God is absolutely the most particular and non-pluralistic aspect of Christianity. As Okholm and Phillips state:

> Dissatisfaction with particularism, especially with its inability to speak more definitively regarding the universal availability of salvation, has produced a massive theological shift in modern theology. Protestant theologians and Catholic theologians after Vatican II have made this a well-trodden path. Christianity is seen as belittling non-Christian religions, which is unacceptable in a multicultural society [built upon] liberal political convictions.[3]

> Pluralists demand that Christians move away from discussing Christ to discussing God.[4]

3. Okholm and Phillips, *Four Views on Salvation*, 24.
4. Okholm and Phillips, *Four Views on Salvation*, 167–68.

Moving away from Christ being God, and just discussing God in general terms, has allowed the perception that all humans with the consciousness of a superior being are basically worshiping the same God. But mix in the incarnation, the full divinity of Jesus Christ, and salvation solely through his life, resurrection, and death, and you're suddenly on dangerous ground. Christianity has undoubtedly changed in order to accommodate modern sensibilities. Most of modern Protestantism now adheres to dispensationalism (with its unapologetic antinomianism, liberalism, and easy believe-ism). And, many Protestant dispensationalists do not even realize that their church is dispensational. Basically, if a church is teaching the rapture, then, in addition to the name on the door, it is also a dispensational church. The entire dispensational system was founded by John Nelson Darby and the Plymouth Brethren in the 1830s (which, ominously, occurred at roughly the same time as the founding of Mormonism). However, a fair number of former dispensationalists are beginning to break ranks and weigh in with some of their objections.

Kyle Idleman states, "Many of our churches in America have gone from being sanctuaries to becoming stadiums. And every week all the fans come to the stadium where they cheer for Jesus but have no interest in truly following him."[5] John MacArthur writes, "As the pressure mounts today to 'contextualize' biblical truth by taming the gospel and toning it down for a self-centered culture, no one should imagine that this reflects some fresh, new, wonderful progressive insight. It is just a new post-modernized version of the no-Lordship gospel."[6] And, finally, the late John Gerstner emphatically declares:

> No matter how many other important truths it proclaims [dispensationalism] cannot be called Christian if it empties Christianity of its essential message. We define a cult as a religion which claims to be Christian while emptying Christianity of that which is essential to it. If dispensationalism does this, then dispensationalism is

5. Idleman, *Not a Fan*, 25.

6. MacArthur, *Gospel According to Jesus*, 10.

a cult and not a branch of the Christian church. It's as serious as that.[7]

> Perhaps most tragic is the false assurance given by dispensationalism to many who have no valid reason to consider themselves Christians. . . . The church is presently faced with a struggle equal in importance to the fourth-century Nicene battle for the deity of Christ.[8]

Lest we think this "toning down of the gospel for a self-centered culture," and "emptying Christianity of that which is essential" is only a modern Protestant manifestation, the February 2019 document signed by Pope Francis and Muslim Iman Ahmed el-Teyeb stated, "The pluralism and diversity of religions are willed by God in his wisdom." Even those Catholics who remained silent during the pope's "loose" same-sex union, homosexual inclusivity, and environmental chatter finally had had enough and began asking if humanist, politically correct Catholicism has gone too far in suggesting that God approves of the existence of false religions. The pope's curious insertion of the word "pluralism" in this 2019 document might also make the 1995 writings of Okholm and Phillips, if not prophetic, at least intuitively anticipatory.

Much more could be said in regard to modern Arianism and what the practical meaning of believing that Jesus Christ is God really involves, but for the purpose of this book, the above overview is sufficient. Along with that thought, I do not wish to distract from the powerful affirmations in chapters 6 and 7 in order to interject a commentary on modern Arianism after each quote. Much of that should be self-evident to the introspective reader. For example, in chapter 6, the deeply committed St. Augustine questions whether playing a musical instrument is a sinful waste of time. This would seem to be an absurd, obsessive concern among today's Christians. However, Bonhoeffer, in his incriminating style, expresses the reason why practitioners of modern "religiosity" might find this concern absurd and unrelated to their own lives when writing:

7. Gertsner, *Wrongly Dividing*, 142.
8. Gertsner, *Wrongly Dividing*, 239, 243.

> The Christian life [has come] to mean nothing more than living in the world as the world [lives], and in being no different from the world. The upshot of all this is that my only duty as a Christian is to leave the world for an hour or so on Sunday and go to church to be assured that my sins are all forgiven.[9]

While there are numerous quotes contained in the next two chapters, I encourage the reader to consider them carefully. Those who read between the lines, and pause to reflect on how their own certainty about Christ being God compares practically to that of St. Augustine and Irenaeus, will find a wealth of introspective treasure to meditate upon. In this age of modern Arianism, that can't possibly be a bad idea, even among those who already embrace christological orthodoxy. Additionally, the preponderance of evidence as to Christ's divinity might provide an incentive for others, including Jehovah's Witnesses, Unitarians, and Mormons, to reevaluate the Arian theology that they have been taught. And finally, the weighty number of quotes underscores the true reason as to why the first three groups perished after there was an accepted list of Bible books. Since it became demonstrably clear that they and their parched theologies were a long way off from the living water of Scripture, they inexorably withered and died.

9. Bonhoeffer, *Cost of Discipleship*, 51.

6

Orthodoxy

Following the debates in the Greek language conducted in the East and only after the first two ecumenical councils, also in the East, the Western Empire became heir to all this valuable information and the fruit of these deliberations. It goes without saying that by extension, every other language that New Testament theology has ever been translated into is also an heir. By one appropriate definition, an heir is anyone "inheriting and continuing the legacy of a predecessor."[1]

What the West and, of course, Rome inherited from the approximately 150 exclusively Eastern bishops was the AD 381 Nicene-Constantinopolitan Creed, which again confirmed the divinity of Christ originally codified at Nicaea, after the chaos, schisms, and, of course, Arianism of the preceding half century. As documented in chapter 4, neither Pope Saint Damasus I of Rome nor his papal legates attended or played any part in the proceedings.

The creed begins:

> We believe in one God, the Father Almighty, Maker of
> heaven and earth, and of all things visible and invisible;

1. See www.dictionary.com.

> And in one Lord Jesus Christ, the Son of God, the Only-begotten, Begotten of the Father before all ages, Light of Light, Very God of Very God, Begotten, not made; of one essence with the Father, by whom all things were made:
>
> Who for us men and for our salvation came down from heaven, and was incarnate of the Holy Spirit and the Virgin Mary, and was made man.[2]

The creed categorically addressed the four fundamental positions about Christ that have been explored throughout this book. In repudiation of the Ebionites, Homoians, Heterousians, and the Arians, it clearly states that Jesus Christ was fully God. In contrast to the Marcionites, it confirms that he was also fully man. Additionally, in addressing at least one form of the multiplicity of Gnostic positions, the creed counters their belief that he was neither God nor man by confirming that he was both. After almost three hundred years of analysis, prayer, and debate, the Greek fathers concluded that Scripture most definitely teaches that Jesus Christ was both fully man and fully God, and the proto-orthodox position became the orthodox position.

As we have already seen, many famous native Greek speakers passed through and even settled in Rome; but by and large, the Latin-speaking Western Roman Empire was at a linguistic disadvantage until St. Jerome completed his translation of the Bible into Latin around AD 405. Even the premier theologian of the Latin world, St. Augustine of Hippo, who many consider to be the greatest extra-biblical writer in Western Christendom, had a limited understanding of Greek. He, of course, had the advantage of the Greek conclusions about the divinity of Christ, but as his writings reflect, he obviously was not fully able to take advantage of the Greek writings of Irenaeus, Athanasius, Gregory of Nazianzus, St. Basil, and many, many other Greek theologians. However, because of his uniquely adept mind, his exceptional secular education in rhetoric, and his later immersion in Scripture under Bishop Ambrose, he produced roughly five million words of original writings

2. *Nicene-Constantinopolitan Creed.*

that have influenced the Catholic Church, the Eastern Church, the Reformation, Calvinism, Lutheranism, the rest of Protestantism, and almost every form of Christianity for the last 1600 years. Although he wrote on virtually everything related to Christianity, his writings on the divinity of Christ are especially exhaustive. It took him almost thirty years to arrive at his conclusions, since he worked on them from AD 400 through 428.[3]

Augustine's literary and intellectual abilities were evident from an early age, but his perspective and outlook were definitely influenced by his highly dysfunctional background. His pagan father wanted him to be a rich and famous intellectual, while his Christian mother, who had an alcohol problem, pushed him toward Christ. Augustine himself openly admitted that he was a slave to his sexual lusts and ultimately fathered an out-of-wedlock child with his longtime mistress. Before becoming fully committed to Christianity, he famously prayed: "God, grant me chastity, but not yet."[4]

Augustine and his lifelong friend Alypius left North Africa together in the mid-380s and arrived in Italy, where Alypius soon developed an insatiable addiction to the Roman blood sports. From his youth, Augustine had observed those close to him worshiping at the hedonist altars of materialism, status, intellectual pride, alcohol, self, and—now with Alypius—brutality and bloodshed, while he himself unapologetically venerated sex and pleasure. He later called all these pursuits "disordered loves" (others have called them "distractions"), and he rightly concluded that "everyone has faith in something because no one has sufficient knowledge. It is not a question of 'Do you have faith?' but of 'What do you put your faith in?'"[5]

The above statement is as true today as it was back then and probably more so, as the list of things in which people put their

---

3. Augustine, *On the Holy Trinity*, 4.

4. Cook and Herzman, "Pick It Up and Read," in *St. Augustine's* Confessions, disc 3, lect. 16, 6:03.

5. Cook and Herzman, *St. Augustine's* Confessions, "A New Look at Christianity," in *St. Augustine's* Confessions, disc 2, lect. 12, 26:45.

faith nowadays is almost limitless. However, belief in these things, as Augustine would soon find out, is premised upon the assumption that tomorrow will be like today. Upon his return to North Africa, that premise was heartbreakingly shattered by the death of his beloved mother, followed by the unexpected death of his adolescent son. He was forced to acknowledge the timeless and uncomfortable fact that yesterday being like today is reliably consistent—until the day it isn't. Christianity and the pagan philosophy of his early schooling intersected after that realization due to the fact that they both encouraged individuals to spend their lives in pursuit of the things that last. He had learned enough of Koine Greek (and now enough of common life) to put into practice the words of Gregory of Nazianzus: "One must chip away the impurities of sin through practices, like fasting, prayer, mastery of the passions [and] meditation on death."[6]

In the process of mastering his passions, Augustine backed out of an arranged marriage (to a ten-year-old girl) during the two years that he had to wait for her to reach the legal age of twelve, as he felt marriage would severely infringe upon the time he would need for what he was beginning to realize was his calling. Upon committing completely to Christianity, Augustine not only put aside his sex addiction but also immersed himself in Scripture and changed his lifestyle so radically that he even questioned if playing a musical instrument was a sinful waste of time. He took the adage "You can't kill time without injuring eternity" to the nth degree. He was to devote the rest of his life, almost unceasingly, to teaching, preaching, and writing.

But before we get to St. Augustine's writings, which scripturally reinforce christological orthodoxy, a little more must be known about the life, contributions, and the essential foundation laid down by another key figure, Athanasius of Alexandria. Also known as Athanasius the Great, he fought against the orthodoxy of his day, which was Arianism.[7] In the Eastern Orthodox Church,

6. Beeley, *Gregory of Nazianzus*, 71.
7. *Great Horologion*, "January 18."

he is labeled as the "Father of Orthodoxy." Some Protestants label him as "Father of the Canon."[8]

Athanasius spent over seventeen years in five exiles ordered by four different Roman emperors, not counting approximately six more incidents in which Athanasius fled Alexandria to escape people seeking to take his life. This gave rise to the expression *Athanasius contra mundum* or "Athanasius against the world."[9]

The widespread Arian opposition to Athanasius was by no means peaceful or civil, as evidenced by the number of times he had to flee for his life and also by the numerous documented cases of proto-orthodox preachers being murdered by the Arians. After one such episode, the murder of Eusebius of Samosata, Gregory of Nazianzus urged his fellow proto-orthodox not to return "violence for violence" in response to these "Arian crimes."[10]

As confirmed in chapter 4, the Council of Nicaea in AD 325 settled nothing. This is clearly evidenced by the fact that Athanasius, who lived from AD 296 through 373, was exiled five times by four different Roman emperors and spent seventeen of the forty-five years he served as bishop of Alexandria in exile. Furthermore, since the last forty-eight years of his life were after the ruling at Nicaea, all of his fleeing and exiles were post-AD 325. He was not appointed bishop of Alexandria until AD 328. Had the issue truly been settled in AD 325 at Nicaea, he would not have become a recognized, authoritative target for the next forty-five years. A biography of Athanasius by the Greek Orthodox Patriarchate of Antioch and All the East corroborates the above: "In the half-century after the First Ecumenical Council held in Nicaea in 325, if there was one man whom the Arians feared and hated more intensely than any other, as being able to lay bare the whole error of their teaching, and to marshal, even from exile or hiding, the beleaguered forces of the orthodox, it was Saint Athanasius the Great."[11]

8. *Great Horologion*, "January 18."

9. Hardy, "St. Athanasius."

10. Beeley, *Gregory of Nazianzus*, 37.

11. *Great Horologion*, "January 18," para. 1.

Arianism was the dominant theology during this period, in spite of Nicaea. Athanasius's book *On the Incarnation*, which he wrote while in his twenties, had helped turn the tide at Nicaea; but like the tide itself, Arianism soon returned. More accurately, it never really receded. Concepts such as those codified at Nicaea can be formulated in short order; but as we have seen, the changing and disproving of a wide range of beliefs is a long, drawn-out, vacillating process.

T. Gilmartin (professor of ecclesiastical history, St. Patrick's College, Maynooth, 1890) confirms much of the above when he writes: "Three hundred bishops assembled in Milan, most from the West, only a few from the East, in 355. They met in the Church of Milan. Shortly, the Emperor ordered them to a hall in the Imperial Palace, thus ending any free debate. He presented an Arian formula of faith for their acceptance. He threatened any who refused with exile and death."[12]

So, thirty years after the Council of Nicaea, some three hundred Western bishops met in Italy, and, by order of the emperor, no debate was allowed; rather, he insisted that Arian theology be accepted under penalty of death. Gilmartin also says of the later Council of Sirmium that "a preliminary conference was held by the Arians at Sirmium, to agree to a formula of faith. A Homoeon creed was adopted, declaring the Son to be 'like the Father.' It was after this Council that Jerome said: 'The whole world groaned in astonishment to find itself Arian.'"[13]

The Council of Sirmium usually

> refers to the third of the four Episcopal councils held in Sirmium between 347 AD and 358 AD. Specifically, one was held in 347, one in 351, one in 357, and one in 358. The third council marked a temporary compromise between Arianism and the Western bishops of the Christian church. At least two of the other councils also dealt primarily with the Arian controversy. All of these

12. Gilmartin, *Manual of Church History*, cited in "Athanasius of Alexandria."

13. Gilmartin, *Manual of Church History*, cited in "Council of Ariminum."

councils were held under the rule of Constantius II, who was sympathetic to the Arians.[14]

Furthermore, as late as 366, one year before his canon was accepted, Athanasius again lost out to the Arians and was exiled: "In October, 364, Athanasius was once more in exile. Two years later, the Emperor Valens, who favored the Arian position, in his turn exiled Athanasius."[15]

In spite of his up-and-down battles against Arianism, the most enduring legacy of Athanasius is the list of canonical books that he believed should be the only authorized books of the New Testament. He said: "In these [twenty-seven writings] alone the teaching of godliness is proclaimed. No one may add to them, and nothing may be taken away from them."[16] This proclamation was monumental, not simply because it is the canon used today but because now every Christian position could be tested against a scriptural standard that all sides agreed beforehand was authoritative. The days of every group endorsing their theology with handpicked, highly edited, and/or outright fraudulent writings were over. There was now a universally accepted benchmark of scriptural "weights and measures," if you will, that standardized what had been random, inconsistent "Christ-trading."

However, the ignorance and illiteracy spoken of in chapter 4 was still a formidable issue. Much like a catchy television jingle today, sailors had been spreading cute little Aryan songs and ditties all over the empire. Just as a short, easily remembered political slogan has greater mass appeal to impatient, easily swayed, ill-informed voters, so Arianism had much more immediate appeal than deep Christology. Widespread cognitive simplicity was not limited to laypeople alone; it was also prevalent among the clergy. Therefore, it was not only the simple-minded laypeople who insisted on the Arian-created Christ, who was small enough to fit comfortably within their minds, but many simple-minded clergy as well. Even

14. "Councils of Sirmium."

15. Clifford, "St. Athanasius."

16. Christian History Magazine Editorial Staff, "Athanasius."

today in our cosmopolitan, largely college-educated society, it is a nearly impossible concept to wrap one's mind around. Among that superstitious, illiterate populace of the ancient Roman Empire, it was an almost insurmountable concept.

St. Augustine contends that the above issue was exactly what Paul was referring to in the second and third chapters of 1 Corinthians:

> For he [Paul] says, "I determined not to know anything among you, save Jesus Christ and him crucified." And a little after that Paul says to them, "And I, brethren, could not speak unto you as unto spiritual, but as unto carnal, even as unto babes in Christ. I fed you with milk, and not meat; for hitherto ye were not able to bear it, neither yet now are ye able."[17]

According to Augustine, the "meat" was the concept of the divinity of Christ that they could not assimilate; the "milk" was an easily understood overview of Christ, his atoning crucifixion, and his relation to their salvation. Paul's mission was not to transform a society of illiterates into a society of theologians but rather to seek and to save the lost among the gentiles, who didn't even have the Jewish background to begin assimilating all this deep Christology. Furthermore, since it took the highly literate, theologically educated, Greek-speaking elders almost three centuries to properly digest this "meat," what chance did these educationally toothless common folk have of consuming it in the time (often brief) before Paul moved on from their town to the next? Absolutely none! Paul recognized that all he would accomplish by introducing the divinity of Christ was to confuse them, to immediately alienate them, and to leave the town no less a pagan bastion than when he arrived.

Augustine goes on to say that "I determined" meant that Paul made a decision not to confuse these gentiles in response to their questions about God, because they were unable to "receive it [and], incapable and wholly unfit to understand."[18] Furthermore, Augustine states that, while these gentiles earnestly inquired about

17. Augustine, *On the Holy Trinity*, 30.
18. Augustine, *On the Holy Trinity*, 18.

the nature of God, what they were anticipating was for the apostle Paul to tell them the details of the very simple, easily understood, Judaistic, singular Jehovah God (which he could not truthfully do). Augustine says that Paul consciously resolved not to introduce his own deep christological understanding (a concept, by the way, that had not been possible for him to understand until meeting Christ on the road to Damascus); and he knew that in telling the gentiles this, they would "not hear what they desire."[19] Augustine's logic, as we shall see, with virtually all of his deeply prayed about and contemplated conclusions, is invariably sound. If the truth of the matter had been that the singular Jewish God was alone to be worshipped—and that's about as complicated as things got—then Paul could have expressed that without any fear of alienating his audience and putting forth something that they could not possibly understand. One all-powerful, Jewish, Old Testament God is a simple, readily understood, easily communicated concept. Paul would not have had to consciously resolve, or determine, or in essence decide to leave out the nature of Christ, move on to other points, and focus on his mission of saving souls and spreading the gospel. Clearly, it was the apostle John's job to explain this deep Christology. As William G. T. Shedd writes, "The apostle John was known among the Primitive church as *ho theologos*, because he was enlightened by the Holy Spirit to make fuller disclosures, in the preface to his gospel, concerning the deity of the Logos."[20] In concert with what multitudes of careful, conscientious theologians have recognized over the millennia, "the Gospel of St. John and particularly the first chapter demonstrates the Divinity of Jesus." The writer then adds: "This Gospel in itself is the greatest support of Athanasius' stand."[21]

Augustine's contention that Paul's focus was on reaching the simple gentiles is exactly what Paul himself spells out in Acts 15:19–20, when he says: "It is my judgment, therefore, that we should not make it difficult for the Gentiles who are turning to

19. Augustine, *On the Holy Trinity*, 18–19.

20. Augustine, *On the Holy Trinity*, 7.

21. Fortescue, "Gospel," 6:662–63.

God. Instead, we should write them telling them to abstain from food polluted by idols, from sexual immorality, from the meat of strangled animals and from blood" (NIV). Had that been all that was required of a mature Christian, the martyrs, as descendants of the pagans whom Paul and the apostles converted, would not have been dying for refusing to worship the emperor and the pagan gods. The simple rules that Paul laid down in the book of Acts were not the end, but merely the beginning of the process of becoming a mature Christian. He himself said "that we should not make it difficult for the Gentiles who are turning to God." Clearly the implication is that he expects them to continue to grow in Christ and to turn toward God with ever greater levels of sincerity, devotion, understanding, and commitment. Not only did the four behavioral admonishments that Paul mentioned in Acts have nothing to do with the divinity of Christ, they had little to do with Christ at all. A faithfully married vegetarian could stay away from pagan blessed or strangled meat, immoral sex, and blood without any Old or New Testament prompts and without any need for anyone's definition of the nature of Christ. Additionally, a great many of those on the earth today would, by those requirements, be considered Christian.

But obviously, much more than those four rules are required to be a Christian. Both East and West realized that the divinity of Christ was the cornerstone of salvation and that without this doctrine, you do not have Christianity. Gregory of Nazianzus reacted to the attempt by the Heterousians to downgrade Christ to an even lower position than Arias had and accused them of arriving at the "logical end" of human rationale.[22] If Christ is not God—and by their continual demotions, the Heterousians had reduced Christ to spiritual insignificance—then whatever religion you have left is certainly not Christianity; they had gutted Christianity of its essence.

Gregory and the proto-orthodox Eastern theologians, while exceptionally brilliant, were too busy addressing and fighting the propositions of the heretics (not to mention the whims and exiles of the emperors) to express things as well as St. Augustine

22. Beeley, *Gregory of Nazianzus*, 21.

did. Augustine had the luxury of writing after all the hard-fought battles over the divinity of Christ had been won by his Greek-speaking predecessors. They were writing from the battlefield, and as soon as one front was subjugated, several more fronts opened up. Augustine could comfortably think, take his time sorting things out (obviously, since it took him twenty-eight years), and then write. That is why his writings are presented in this chapter, but that certainly does not mean that they are easy to understand. Dr. South's oft-repeated quip is indeed accurate: "As he that denies this fundamental article of Christian religion may lose his soul, so he that much strives to understand it may lose his wits."[23]

One of the first scriptural points that St. Augustine makes was also made by the Greek theologians. Reading the same Bible and coming up with similar conclusions on some verses would be logical and not evidence of copycatting. If there's anything that Augustine was, it was original. Basically, Augustine contends that an eternal Father implies an eternal Son, as the very term *Father* is meaningless if not in relation to a Son. Therefore, no Son, no Father.[24] Scripture teaches that the Father is such from eternity, which rules out the possibility of the unchangeable God changing into something else after creating the Son—if that were the case. And if the Son were created, "the Father" had some other designation before that event and is not the eternal Father of Scripture. This is even recognized in Islam. Among the ninety-nine or so names used for their monad God "Allah," father is not one of them, as that, they accurately assess, would denote something other than a strict, singular monad.

Next, his commentary on 1 Cor 1:24 is self-explanatory: "The Son of God is the power and the wisdom of God, and God was never without power and wisdom. . . . A man must be senseless to say that God at any time had not power and wisdom; therefore, there was no time when the Son was not."[25]

<hr>

23. Augustine, *On the Holy Trinity*, 3.
24. Augustine, *On the Holy Trinity*, 6.
25. Augustine, *On the Holy Trinity*, 97.

In his commentary on Phil 2:6, Augustine states: "It is also said of the Son, 'He thought it not robbery to be equal with God.' We ask, equal according to what? For if He is not said to be equal according to substance, then they admit that something may be said of God not according to substance."[26] Augustine rhetorically asks his reader to name a characteristic of the pure Spirit Father that is not intrinsic to his nature. This attribute would have to be either physical, superficial, or superfluous, of which some created being could be said to share equally in it with him. He wants his reader to ponder this and try to identify some aspect where a created Christ, or any created being, could say, "I am equal with God," because, for instance, we are the same height. Like the same Bible verses? Have a fondness for Jerusalem? Even Satan, probably the highest order of created being we are aware of, knew that equality with God in any way was impossible; thus, we are told in Isa 14:14 that he said, "I will make myself like the most high" (NIV). After one exhausts oneself trying to find even one thing where he or she or any created being can claim equality with God, Augustine confirms that a created Christ, or anything created is incapable of being "equal in anything." He then retorts, "But Scripture proclaims, that 'He thought it not robbery to be equal with God.'" Therefore, if "the Son is equal with God [in] one thing . . . He is equal in all things."[27]

Augustine's next thought, on Gen 1:26, where God says, "Let us make man in our image, after our likeness," has also been echoed by many others. But the gist is, since it is written to Jewish monotheists who believed in only one Creator, Augustine's contention is that if Christ were not a co-equal, co-creator, this would have been written, "Let me make man in my image, after my likeness."[28] Augustine's point is that creation was a pretty big deal and that if Christ were not equally responsible for the creation with the Father and not merely the instrument of creation, as some contend, it would be written as Augustine says. A less than perfect example is how in modern times, the credit for an exceptional

26. Augustine, *On the Holy Trinity*, 88.
27. Augustine, *On the Holy Trinity*, 99.
28. Augustine, *On the Holy Trinity*, 5.

building goes to the illustrious architect and not to the head of the construction crew. If a famous building had a plaque out front that said "made by Frank Lloyd Wright and Joe Smith," it would be clear that Joe Smith was more than just the head of the construction crew. Worded like that, the plaque would intimate that Frank and Joe equally take credit for the project, just as "let us make man in our image" does.

His next analysis, concerning Abraham's three visitors, is not so generic, and his own words are again self-explanatory:

> The beginning of that narrative does not say, three men appeared to him, but, "The LORD appeared to him . . ." Abraham invites [them] to his hospitality in the plural number, and afterwards speaks to them in the singular number as one; and as one He promises him a son. . . . Three men appeared to him; no one of whom is said to have stood prominently above the others, no one more than the others to have shown with greater glory, or to have acted more authoritatively? . . . Why should we not here understand, as visibly intimated by the creature . . . equality . . . and one in the same substance in the persons.[29]

> The theophanies of the Pentateuch [teach the equality of the Father and Son] in their implication. They involve distinctions in God—God sending and God sent; God speaking of God, and God speaking to God.[30]

The next Old Testament example that Augustine cites, the seventh chapter of Daniel, raises a myriad of complicated questions:

> One like the Son of Man came with the clouds of heaven, and came to the Ancient of Days, and they brought Him near before Him. And there was given Him dominion, and glory, and a kingdom, and all peoples, nations and languages, should serve Him; His dominion is an everlasting dominion, which shall not pass away, and His

29. Augustine, *On the Holy Trinity*, 46–47.

30. Augustine, *On the Holy Trinity*, 47.

> kingdom that which shall not be destroyed. Behold the
> Father giving, and the Son receiving an eternal kingdom.[31]

Clearly Christ and the Father are pictured here, but strangely, everyone on earth, without exception, is commanded to worship Christ, thereby raising two dilemmas. The point emphasized earlier by Gregory of Nazianzus about serving only God is again raised here since, undeniably, Christ is to be served. Furthermore, if everyone on earth is serving Christ for eternity, then who is left to serve God? The question of the kingdom leads into his next commentary.

Augustine explains what Paul is teaching about Christ handing the kingdom over to the Father in 1 Cor 15:24:

> Neither may we think that Christ shall so give up the kingdom to God, even the Father, as that He shall take it away from himself. For some vain talkers have thought even this. For when it is said, He shall have delivered up the kingdom to God, even the Father, He himself is not excluded; because He is one God together with the Father. But that word "until" deceives those who are careless readers of the Divine Scriptures, but eager for controversy. For the text continues, for He must reign until he hath put all enemies under His feet, as though, when He had put them, He would no more reign?[32]

Augustine again rhetorically asks the "careless readers" whether, consistent with their theology, they then believe that the Father does not have the kingdom right now? He also reminds them that Christ will reign forever and ever, and that his kingdom is an everlasting kingdom, which makes their postulations untenable.

Next, Augustine gives a somewhat wordy explanation of the first chapter of the Gospel of John, which he calls "the most plain and unanimous voice of divine testimonies."[33] He proceeds to say:

31. Augustine, *On the Holy Trinity*, 53.

32. Augustine, *On the Holy Trinity*, 25.

33. Augustine, *On the Holy Trinity*, 21.

"In the beginning was the Word, and the Word was with God, and the Word was God." But herein is declared, not only that He is God, but also that He is of the same substance with the Father; because, after saying, "And the Word was God," it is said also, "The same was in the beginning with God: all things were made by Him, and without Him was not anything made." Not simply "all things"; but only all things that were made, that is, the whole creature. From which it appears clearly that He Himself was not made by whom all things were made. And if He was not made, then He is not creature; but if He is not creature, then He is of the same substance with the Father. For all substance that is not God is creature; and all that is not creature is God. And if the Son is not the same substance with the Father, then He is a substance that was made: and if He is a substance that was made, all things were not made by Him; but "all things were made by Him," therefore He is of one and the same substance with the Father. And so, He is not only God, but also very God.[34]

Many would say that if there is one definitive affirmation of the divinity of Christ in the Bible, this is it. As Augustine says, it's pretty clear. Many theologians say that the entire Gospel of John hammers home the divinity of Christ in every way possible from beginning to end and culminates with Christ calmly accepting being addressed by Thomas as "My Lord and my God." But in regard to just the first chapter, Irenaeus, the disciple of Polycarp, who was the disciple of John, also says that this is pretty clear and definitive. He writes in *Against Heresies*, that "all things were made by Him, and without Him was nothing made. There is no exception or deduction stated."[35]

Augustine continues, "But if all things were made by the Father and all things by the Son, then the same things were made by

34. Augustine, *On the Holy Trinity*, 21–22.
35. Irenaeus, *Against Heresies*, bk 1, 347.

the Father and by the Son. The Son, therefore, is equal with the Father, and the working of the Father and the Son is indivisible."[36]

Those who wish to deny that this means exactly what it says must in their commentaries make an exception or deduction by interjecting the word "other" and thus make John's Gospel read, "All [other] things were made by him"; and in so doing they put their understandings above God's understandings and proceed to "correct" God. On top of this, when God retorts back that it is they who do not understand by reemphasizing the point emphatically and declaring "and without Him was not anything made that was made"; rather than humbly taking the reprimand and then reconsidering their own position, they actually insist on their theological superiority over that of the Creator of the universe. Moreover, further compounding the affront, they not only get into an argument with God (by their insertions), but imply that his communication skills are lacking in that God is not capable of accurately expressing what he really means (twice in a row, mind you) without the aid of their commentary. Lest we think that this kind of arrogance is limited to the so-called cults, it has become mainstream nowadays, as everywhere it is being taught that in many obvious instances, God really meant to say the exact opposite of what he said, or that in this part of the New Testament he is talking to others and not to you generous tithers sitting here today.

Kyle Idleman, in his book *Not a Fan*, provides an interesting example of the above:

> Do you remember reading the story in the news about the conviction of a pharmacist named Robert Courtney? He was convicted of diluting the medication of cancer patients in order to make a profit. Over a period of about nine years he diluted an estimated 98,000 prescriptions of medications affecting some 42,000 patients. At least 17 cancer patients died after receiving diluted formulation of chemotherapy. He made some 19 million dollars from the fraud. Robert was sentenced to 30 years in prison. A man had been entrusted with the responsibility of

36. Augustine, *On the Holy Trinity*, 23.

handing out life-saving medication; but for the sake of personal gain diluted it to the point where it couldn't help people. That's a picture of what many preachers, including myself, are sometimes guilty of doing.[37]

Obviously, this short sampling of Augustine's writings can only provide a brief overview of his over five hundred pages of writing and twenty-eight years of prayerful contemplation on the divinity of Christ; however, the last concept of his that I will share in this chapter is one that he uses in many different places to explain apparent contradictions. Augustine says that we must be aware when Christ is talking in some places as man, since he is fully man, and in other places as God, since he is fully God. He says that when Christ emptied himself, not only did he become less than God, even though he was God, but also, he became less than himself. Thus, Augustine explains the apparent contradictions between, on one hand, Jesus saying "The Father is greater than I," and on the other hand, "I and the Father are One"—and to Philip "He that hath seen Me has seen the Father."[38] He writes:

> For in the form of a servant which He took He is less than the Father; but in the form of God, in which also He was before He took the form of a servant, He was equal to the Father. In the form of God, He is the Word, "by whom all things are made," but in the form of a servant He was made of a woman, made under the law, to redeem them that are under the law. In like manner, in the form of God He made man; in the form of a servant He was made man.[39]

Augustine also goes on to explain that in the form of a servant, "He is less than the Holy Spirit, because He Himself says, 'Whosoever speaketh a word against the Son of man, it shall be forgiven him; but whosoever speaketh against the Holy Ghost, it shall not be forgiven him.'"[40]

37. Idleman, *Not a Fan*, 165–166.

38. Augustine, *On the Holy Trinity*, 24, 26.

39. Augustine, *On the Holy Trinity*, 24.

40. Augustine, *On the Holy Trinity*, 29–30.

Augustine defines this as a rule for properly interpreting Scripture. Depending on what form the Son is speaking in, Creator or servant, he is either equal with God or less than God (and thereby less than himself). This dichotomy is evidenced even when Christ is speaking on subjects not overtly related to his nature, as when he says in some places that he will not judge but then in other places says, "The father judgeth no man, but hath committed all judgment to the Son." It is a blatant contradiction, unless it is as Augustine writes: "I will not judge, but I will judge? How can this be true, unless it is this way: I will not judge by human power [but through] reverting to the Godhead."[41]

Another place where Augustine uses his rule for properly interpreting Scripture is in Prov 8:23–31, as an argument against those who say that this teaches a created Christ. However, other writers seem to contest this premise in fewer, clearer words than Augustine. The *Cambridge Bible for Schools and Colleges* says:

> This word has been a battleground of controversy since the days of the Arian heresy. But it is well to remember that, all theological questions apart, it is impossible to understand the word, whatever rendering of it we adopt, as indicating that Wisdom ever had a beginning, or was ever properly speaking created. Wisdom is inseparable from any worthy conception of Him who is "the only wise God" (1 Timothy 1:17), and therefore is like Him "from everlasting to everlasting" (Psalm 90:1)."[42]

The *Cambridge Bible* contends that wisdom could never have had a "beginning" and always has been an essential foundational trait "inseparable" from the eternal God. This, of course, echoes St. Augustine's prior statement that "a man must be senseless to say that God at any time had not power and wisdom."[43]

Additionally, Wheaton College Professor Leland Ryken says that this is clearly a poetic personification:

41. Augustine, *On the Holy Trinity*, 32–34.

42. Findlay, *Cambridge Bible for Schools*, cited in Bible Hub, "Proverbs 8:22."

43. Augustine, *On the Holy Trinity*, 97.

> How can you know when a poet has used personification? It is not complicated: whenever a poet attributes human qualities to something inanimate, often an abstraction, he or she has used personification. . . . This takes us back to Proverbs 8. The main subject of Proverbs chapters 1–9 is wisdom, which is an abstract quality or character trait rather than a person, but wisdom is treated as a woman from the first chapter right through chapter 9. Wisdom is portrayed as a woman of dazzling attractiveness and virtue, who teaches in the marketplace of the town (1:20), who is romantically embraced (4:8–9), who can be addressed as "my sister" (7:4), who utters a long speech commending herself to the public (chapter 8). . . . Interpreters have done a lot of mischief by taking figurative language literally. . . . The speaker is wisdom personified. Those who press for a literal interpretation of Proverbs 8 face the daunting task of explaining why the pronoun and language used for wisdom are feminine—is Christ feminine in His true essence or does He have a female counterpart in heaven to whom this passage refers?[44]

Ryken goes on to intimate that it is impossible to carry out this allegory through all nine chapters of Proverbs, where wisdom is spoken of as a female. If you consistently interject Christ throughout the first nine chapters of Proverbs, many of the thirty-plus verses where wisdom/Christ is referred to as a female become completely nonsensical. Are we to gain a new understanding of Christ as our sister? In regard to 8:12, are we to assume that Christ as wisdom literally dwells in heaven with another person named "Prudence"? Even more interesting is the fact that those who hold this interpretation blatantly contradict the clear teaching in the first chapter of John, where Christ is unequivocally declared to be God, and build their theology on this allegorical poem. Unless one is a Gnostic, who believes that Christ is both a male and female dyad, the interjection of Christ in the dozens of verses where wisdom is said to be female is rationally unsustainable. To do so while changing the

44. Ryken, "Who Is Wisdom in Proverbs 8?"

crystal clear meaning of the first chapter of John's Gospel is clearly a case of literalizing the allegorical and allegorizing the literal.

Finally, even after decades of in-depth study, St. Augustine was still in awe of the incomprehensibility of the subject and shared a little perspective on how to come to grips with a concept that is inconceivable to the human mind. He directs us toward a familiar incomprehensibility, which we readily accept, by astutely asserting that we don't reject the eternal existence of God just because we can't think in those terms; rather, we accept it because Scripture teaches it. He put the divinity of Christ in the same category and asks, "Which of the two is the most baffling?" He goes on to say that "no theist rejects the doctrine of Divine eternity because of its mystery. The two doctrines are antithetic and correlative."[45]

45. Augustine, *On the Holy Trinity*, 10–11.

7

Back to the Fountainhead

We know that Paul and many of the New Testament writers had others in their intimate circle who were their scribes and actually did the physical writing of their New Testament words. At the end of 1 Corinthians, Colossians, and other letters, Paul makes a point of saying, "I, Paul, write this greeting in my own hand," clearly informing us that somebody else physically wrote the body of the letter. Paul Boer, in his book on St. Ignatius, tells us that "it is also believed, and with great probability, that, with his friend Polycarp, he [Ignatius] was among the auditors of the Apostle St. John."[1] Boer is apprising us of the widespread contention that Polycarp was part of the inner circle that did the physical writing of John's New Testament words. This is quite "probable," as Boer says, since many sources confirm that Polycarp was with John during the time John is believed to have written. Professor Paul Hartog writes that "Polycarp occupies an important place in the history of the early Christian Church."[2] Philip Schaff adds that

> he is among the earliest Christians whose writings survived. Saint Jerome wrote that Polycarp was a

1. Boer, *St. Ignatius of Antioch*, 11.
2. Hartog, *Polycarp's Epistle*, 86.

> "disciple of the apostle John and by him ordained bishop
> of Smyrna." He was an elder of an important congrega-
> tion which was a large contributor to the founding of the
> Christian Church.[3]

According to David Trobisch, author of *Who Published the New Testament*, "Polycarp may have been the one who compiled, edited, and published the New Testament."[4] All of the above gets us as close to the fountainhead as one can get and, if Polycarp was the actual author of John's writings or did actually publish the New Testament, then in Polycarp we have someone who actually dipped his pen in the Gospel's living water.

However, even if he were not the actual scribe, it is inconceivable that he could have been taught by John and the other apostles—which he inarguably was—and in their company for years, without getting a very clear and explicit explanation regarding some of the most breathtakingly shocking verses in the entire Bible. In those verses, John confirms that Jesus Christ is the very God of both the Old and New Testaments. We know that Polycarp received minutely specific instruction regarding the divinity of Christ, not only because it would be inconceivable that a theologian could spend years with John and the apostles and not have this fundamental concept thoroughly explained to him but also because of how strongly Irenaeus, the disciple whom Polycarp taught, reinforces the equality of Christ with God the Father. I daresay that I have never heard anyone declare the Son's equality with the Father so boldly, as you shall see, and it is almost unprecedented that someone would venture to relay that particular humanly incomprehensible concept with such unambiguous certainty and conviction. He writes as if Christ were sitting right next to him proofreading his commentaries for accuracy; and, if all of the above is true, which is likely, that picture is probably not an excessively unrealistic magnification.

There are other assertions that Irenaeus makes that we accept today, not only as absolute fact but as the bedrock of scriptural

3. Roberts et al., *Nicene and Post-Nicene Fathers*, 3:788.
4. Tobisch, "Who Published New Testament," 30.

authenticity itself. For instance, in their book *The Canon Debate*, McDonald and Sanders point out that "Irenaeus is also the earliest attestation that the Gospel of John was written by John the Apostle and that the Gospel of Luke was written by Luke, the companion of Paul."[5] Furthermore, in *Against Heresies*, Irenaeus quotes from virtually every book in our current New Testament nearly two centuries before it was accepted as canon. He did leave out a few of the very shortest New Testament books, but biblical historians suggest that they were missing due only to their limited words and content. Nevertheless, he had to have been told which books were authentic by Polycarp, who was obviously told by John, and some 1800 years later virtually all of us accept and recite what Irenaeus believed to be apostolically sanctioned New Testament Scripture.

The fact that it was Polycarp who directed him to only those books and also taught him his theology and Christology makes him about as close to the source of truth as is humanly possible. It also makes it clear that anyone contradicting his assertions must have a rock-solid, airtight, error-free scriptural argument; and, as we have seen with even a small sampling of St. Augustine's thirty-year investigation of the subject, he punches holes in any counterclaims that are irrefutable. Therefore, no argument against the divinity of Christ can be said to be scripturally airtight and rock solid. There is also the track record of some 1600 years and thousands upon thousands of devoted theologians who could have contradicted the Nicene and Constantinople Creeds but instead found them to be scriptural. Thus, any individuals claiming that Christ is not God are proclaiming themselves the premier theologians of the last two millennia and reducing all those thousands who preceded them to misdirected simpletons.

Most who deny the divinity of Christ can trace their particular theology or denomination back only a century or two. Irenaeus links his theology back to Christ himself. Moreover, while the leaders of almost all modern denominations may see themselves as a link between Christ and the laypeople in a figurative sense,

---

5. McDonald and Sanders, *Canon Debate*, 267.

Irenaeus is a genuine link between Christ and us in an absolute literal sense (see figure 1).

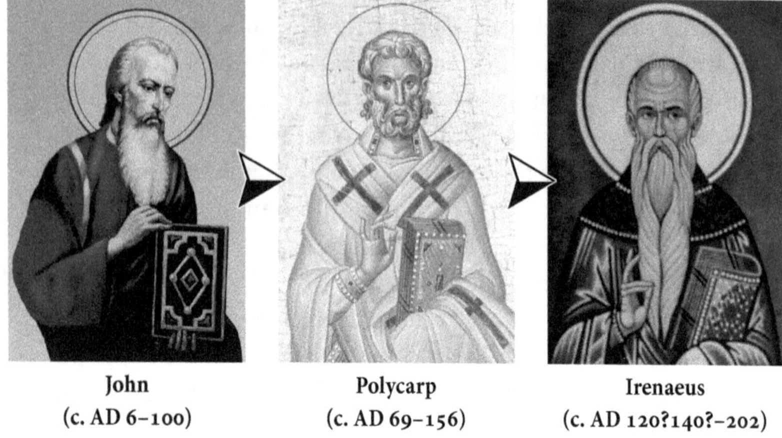

John
(c. AD 6–100)

Polycarp
(c. AD 69–156)

Irenaeus
(c. AD 120?140?–202)

**Figure 1. There are only two degrees of separation
between the apostle John and Irenaeus.**

The words of Irenaeus should weigh heavily on those who would consider themselves followers of Christ. I say "should" because once you factor in human nature, changing a lifelong direction and thought pattern becomes a near impossibility. Justin Martyr addresses this issue when he says "we are well aware that it is not easy suddenly to change a mind possessed by ignorance." He goes on to say that he speaks what he knows anyway because some hearts are fertile soil possessed by individuals who, above everything else, "love the truth." And while Justin Martyr knew that most of his words would fall by the wayside, as did the majority of his Lord's words, he also knew that there were likely to be at least a few receptive hearts. Therefore, his hope was to be able to put "ignorance to flight by presenting the truth."[6]

In discerning the truth regarding the nature of Christ, the simplest, least enigmatic, most comfortable understanding would be that of a created Christ. In her best-selling book *A History of God*, Karen Armstrong addresses the debate about whether

6. Justin Martyr, *First and Second Apologies*, 9.

Christ belonged to the divine realm or the fragile created order. Besides outlining some of the early Christian debates, she makes two thought-provoking statements relating to the desire that we all have to embrace a God we can understand. The first of these was that "Islam spread with astonishing rapidity throughout the Middle East and Africa. Many of its enthusiastic converts in these lands—where Hellenism was not on home ground—turned with relief from Greek Trinitarianism, which expressed the mystery of God in an idiom that was alien to them."[7] She also writes that "when Christians in the West became embarrassed by this dogma during the eighteenth century and tried to jettison it, they were trying to make God rational and comprehensible to the Age of Reason."[8] Additionally, the Nazi-era "Positive Christianity" mentioned earlier in the book also demonstrates that a superficial, humanly reasoned assessment of Scripture hastily settles on a Christ who can't be God (as the Nazis were not exactly painstakingly attentive theologians).

The belief that Christ is God has never been a comfortable, readily understood doctrine, yet it has endured because, despite its incomprehensibility, it is taught in Scripture. It is not a simple concept, as evidenced by the fact that St. Augustine studied the divinity of Christ for thirty years before he felt qualified to write about it. Some of those who deny the divinity of Christ have oversimplified the issue, built a theology on a few nebulous verses, and then found themselves saddled with the huge task of rewriting and reinterpreting a great deal of Scripture from one end of the Bible to the other in order to scrub it up so that it conforms to their simplistic conclusions. Like any of us who joined a church denomination when we were young, not only were we at the mercy of the doctrines of our teachers and organizations, but also, we excluded God's Spirit and personal spiritual growth from the teaching process until it was much too late to undo what we had learned. From that point on, our Scripture reading was less a search for God's truth and more a quest for confirmation of the things we

7. Armstrong, *History of God*, 118.
8. Armstrong, *History of God*, 131.

had already assimilated. Consequently, for all the above reasons, going back as close to the fountainhead as is possible cannot be a bad idea for any truth seeker. The term *truth seeker* applies to all, even those who accept Christ's divinity. Most who believe in the doctrine cannot even describe it coherently or consistently. Therefore, because even they are not sure what they believe, the bold, unambiguous words of Irenaeus should prove illuminating to all.

From cover to cover, all five hundred pages of *Against Heresies* are one confirmation after another of the equality of Christ with the Father. In countering the other three "Christian" groups, Irenaeus comes back to that affirmation time and time again. I wish to highlight the fact that Irenaeus continually endorses the apostle John and his disciple Polycarp's conviction that Christ is God. I point this out because the Gnostics and the Marcionites were not the only ones who twisted and perverted Scripture. Many who reject the divinity of Christ have been told that, like the aforementioned two groups, ancient proto-orthodox writings have also been doctored. This is certainly true in the case of St. Ignatius of Antioch, as there are long and short versions of his epistles that are contradictory. Obviously, one or both of the two versions are ripe with interpolations, which is just a fancy term for rewriting things after the fact to get them to say what you want them to say. That kind of interpolation is virtually impossible with Irenaeus, as he speaks in such depth and detail that his paragraphs would be totally incoherent if someone tried to edit his carefully crafted words. On top of that, there are many antique commentaries, rebuttals, and other writings that confirm the authenticity of his words. Refreshingly, but not coincidentally, he uses only the books that will eventually become the accepted canon of Scripture.

Quite definitively, Irenaeus states that

> because the Son of God is implanted everywhere throughout [Moses's] writings: at one time, indeed speaking with Abraham, and about to eat with him; at another time with Noah, giving to him the dimensions of the ark; at another inquiring after Adam; at another, bringing down judgment upon the Sodomites; and again

when He becomes visible, and directs Jacob on his journey, and speaks with Moses from the Bush, and it would
be endless to recount the occasions upon which the son
of God is shown forth by Moses.[9]

So, in all of the above instances, where the Tetragrammaton
is used (Yhwh, Lord), Irenaeus is saying that it was the Son of
God. Therefore, it was Jesus Christ who spoke to Moses from
the bush, appeared to Abraham, and also gave the instructions
about the building of the ark to Noah. Irenaeus is telling us in
no uncertain terms that everywhere in the five books of Moses
where the Tetragrammaton is used, as in the Lord, Yahweh, or
Jehovah, it is Jesus Christ speaking. Simply reading the Penta-
teuch and substituting "Jesus Christ" in every place where it says
"the Lord" will graphically underlie the explicit, unmistakable
contention of his words.

Irenaeus could not make things any clearer or straightforward than when he writes: "For the Father is the invisible of the
Son, but the Son is the visible of the Father. And for this reason all
speak with Christ when He was present on earth, and they named
him God. . . . While He received testimony from all that He was
very man, and that He was very God."[10]

There are just too many pages in his book where Irenaeus
plainly and unreservedly claims that Jesus Christ is the Jehovah
God of the Old Testament. Short of writing a hundred-page chapter, I could not even begin to encompass them all. That being said,
the following small sequential sampling will have to suffice:

> In order that to Christ Jesus, our Lord, and God, and
> Savior, and King, according to the will of the invisible
> Father, "every knee should bow."[11]

> But God being all mind, and all Logos, both speaks exactly
> what He thinks, and thinks exactly what He speaks.[12]

9. Irenaeus, *Against Heresies*, bk 4, 473.
10. Irenaeus, *Against Heresies*, bk 4, 469.
11. Irenaeus, *Against Heresies*, bk 1, 330.
12. Irenaeus, *Against Heresies*, bk 2, 400.

> But the Son, eternally co-existing with the Father, from of old, yea, from the beginning . . .[13]

> And again, when the Son speaks to Moses, he says, "I [the LORD] am come down to deliver this people."[14]

> They showed, by these gifts which they offered, who it was that was worshipped; myrrh, because it was He who should die and be buried for the mortal human race; gold, because He was a King, "of whose kingdom is no end"; and frankincense, because he was God.[15]

> But inasmuch as He was God, He did not judge according to glory.[16]

> But in every respect, too, He is man, the formation of God; and thus, He took a man onto himself, the invisible becoming visible, the incomprehensible being made comprehensible.[17]

> For I have shown that the Son of God did not [at the incarnation] begin to exist, being with the Father from the beginning; but [that's] when He became incarnate and was made man.[18]

> It is from that region which is towards the south of the inheritance of Judah that the Son of God shall come, who is God, and was from Bethlehem, where the Lord was born.[19]

---

13. Irenaeus, *Against Heresies*, bk 2, 406.
14. Irenaeus, *Against Heresies*, bk 3, 419.
15. Irenaeus, *Against Heresies*, bk 3, 423.
16. Irenaeus, *Against Heresies*, bk 3, 423.
17. Irenaeus, *Against Heresies*, bk 3, 443.
18. Irenaeus, *Against Heresies*, bk 3, 446.
19. Irenaeus, *Against Heresies*, bk 3, 451.

> For He who uttered [such words] was Truth and did truly
> vindicate His own house by driving out of it the chang-
> ers of the money, who were buying and selling, saying to
> them: "It is written, My house shall be called a house of
> prayer; but ye have made it a den of thieves."[20]

The above overview barely scratches the surface of what Irenaeus wrote in *Against Heresies* about Christ's equality with the
Father. The sampling of sequential quotes is devoid of commentary because Irenaeus speaks so well for himself that it would be
counterproductive and superfluous to interrupt.

Irenaeus understood that by design this life is replete with
obstacles, turmoil, painful choices, and endless distractions, where
people are continually challenged to make moral decisions and to
set eternal rather than ephemeral priorities—because only through
difficulties and the judicious use of time can we grow spiritually
and become mature moral agents. Knowing this, Irenaeus would
neither bow to nor serve the gods of the hedonists, the gods of
the heretics, or any god but Christ, because he had no delusions
about what awaited him as a human being and he recognized
that everything in this short life is but a thin veneer. Consistent
with his expectations, he is believed to have been martyred for his
faith during the reign of Emperor Septimius Severus somewhere
around AD 202.

Irenaeus had spent virtually his entire adult life as an in-
domitable heresiologist astutely countering everything that went
against the christological teachings of the apostle John and Polycarp. While the concept of Christ being the true God of both the
Old and New Testaments is impossible to humanly comprehend
and the profusion of scriptural evidence is too theologically deep
to easily comprehend, the crystal clear definitive statements by
Irenaeus are impossible *not* to comprehend. And, as emphasized
throughout this chapter, by being a mere two steps removed from
the apostle John, the writings of Irenaeus are as close to the fountainhead of truth as one can possibly get.

20. Irenaeus, *Against Heresies*, bk 4, 464.

The Battle for the Divinity of Christ in the Early Centuries

Almost two thousand years later, at a time when fundamental Christian doctrines are being rejected based upon the flimsiest of evidence, the core conviction that Jesus Christ is the true God of Scripture is also under attack, both overtly and covertly. It is therefore a fitting time to deeply reflect on the lives and words of Irenaeus and all of the other faithful, prayerful servants of God noted in this book, who allowed nothing in the temporal to distract them from the eternal. Heretics, hardships, and even the unrelenting might of the Roman Empire could not derail them as they fought the early battles for the divinity of Christ with their faith, their pens, and their blood.

Bibliography

Armstrong, Karen. *A History of God: The 4,000-Year Quest of Judaism, Christianity and Islam.* New York: Ballantine, 2011.

"Athanasius of Alexandria." Wikipedia, last edited Jan. 27, 2023. https://en.wikipedia.org/wiki/Athanasius of Alexandria.

Athanasius of Alexandria. *On the Incarnation.* North Charleston, SC: CreateSpace, 2016.

Augustine. *The City of God and the City of Man.* Translated by Marcus Dods. Boston: Digireads, 2017.

———. *On the Holy Trinity, Doctrinal Treatises, Moral Treatises.* Edited by Philip Schaff. Revised and Annotated, with an Introductory Essay by William G. T. Shedd. Vol. 3 of *Nicene and Post-Nicene Fathers,* 1st ser. Buffalo: Christian Literature, 1887.

Barnstone, Willis. *The Other Bible.* New York: HarperCollins, 2005.

Beeley, Christopher A. *Gregory of Nazianzus on the Trinity and the Knowledge of God: In Your Light We Shall See Light.* Oxford Studies in Historical Theology. New York: Oxford University Press, 2008.

Bible Hub. "Proverbs 8:22." Bible Hub, n.d. https://biblehub.com/commentaries/proverbs/8-22.htm.

Boer, Paul. *St. Ignatius of Antioch: The Epistles.* North Charleston, SC: CreateSpace, 2012.

Bonhoeffer, Dietrich. *The Cost of Discipleship.* Translated by R. H. Fuller; revised by Irmgard Booth. New York: Touchstone, 1995.

Brons, David. "A Brief Summary of Valentinian Theology." Gnostic Society Library, n.d. http://gnosis.org/library/valentinus/Brief_Summary_Theology.htm.

Christian History Magazine Editorial Staff. "Athanasius." *Christianity Today,* n.d. From *131 Christians Everyone Should Know,* edited by Mark Galli and Ted Olsen, Holman Reference (Nashville: Broadman & Holman, 2000). https://www.christianitytoday.com/history/people/theologians/athanasius.html.

Bibliography

Clifford, C. "St. Athanasius." New Advent, n.d. From vol. 2 of *The Catholic Encyclopedia* (New York: Appleton, 1907). http://www.newadvent.org/cathen/02035a.htm.

Cook, William R., and Ronald B. Herzman. *St. Augustine's* Confessions. Great Courses. Chantilly, VA: Teaching Company, 2004. DVD.

"Council of Ariminum." Wikipedia, last edited Aug. 23, 2022. https://en.wikipedia.org/wiki/Council_of_Ariminum.

"Councils of Sirmium." Wikipedia, last edited Feb. 3, 2022. https://en.wikipedia.org/wiki/Councils_of_Sirmium.

Cross, F. L., ed. *The Oxford Dictionary of the Christian Church*. New York: Oxford University Press, 2005.

Daily Catholic. "Major Councils of the Church." Daily Catholic, n.d. http://www.dailycatholic.org/councils.htm.

Dillon, Matthew J. "Gnosticism Theorized: Major Trends and Approaches to the Study of Gnosticism." In *Religion: Secret Religion*, edited by April D. DeConick, 23–28. New York: Macmillan, 2016.

Dunn, James D. G. "The Apostle of the Heretics?" In *The Language and Literature of the New Testament: Essays in Honor of Stanley E. Porter's 60th Birthday*, edited by Lois Fuller Dow et al., Biblical Interpretation 150, 521–35. Leiden, Neth.: Brill, 2016.

Ehrman, Bart M. *Lost Christianities: The Battles for Scripture and the Battles over Authentication*. Chantilly, VA: Teaching Company, 2002. DVD.

Eusebius. *The History of the Church*. Translated by Arthur Cushman McGiffert. Boston: Digireads, 2018.

Findlay, George Gillanders. *Cambridge Bible for Schools and Colleges*. London: Forgotten, 2018.

Fortescue, Adrian. "Gospel." In *The Catholic Encyclopedia*, 6:662–63. New York: Appleton, 1907.

Gertsner, John H. *Wrongly Dividing the Word of Truth: A Critique of Dispensationalism*. 3rd ed. Draper, VA: Nicene Council, 2009.

Gilmartin, T. *Manual of Church History*. Dublin: Gill & Son, 1890.

"Gnosticism." Wikipedia, last edited Jan. 28, 2023. https://en.wikipedia.org/wiki/Gnosticism.

Great Horologion. "January 18: Our Fathers among the Saints Athanasius and Cyril, Archbishops of Alexandria." Year of Our Salvation, n.d. From *Great Horologion* (Brookline, MA: Holy Transfiguration Seminary, 1997). http://tyoos.org/Lives-of-Saints/January/Jan-18/SS-Athanasius-Cyril.html#:~:text=In%20the%20half%2Dcentury%20after,the%20Orthodox%2C%20it%20was%20Saint.

Hardy, Edward R. "St. Athanasius." *Encyclopædia Britannica*, Sept. 9, 2022. https://www.britannica.com/biography/Saint-Athanasius.

Harris, Stephen L. *Understanding the Bible*. Palo Alto, CA: Mayfield, 1985.

Hartog, Paul, ed. *Polycarp's Epistle to the Philippians and the Martyrdom of Polycarp*. Oxford: Oxford University Press, 2013.

Idleman, Kyle. *Not a Fan: Becoming a Completely Committed Follower of Jesus.* Grand Rapids: Zondervan, 2009.

"Irenaeus." Wikipedia, last edited Jan. 17, 2023. https://en.wikipedia.org/wiki/Irenaeus.

Irenaeus. *Against Heresies.* Edited by Alexander Roberts and James Donaldson. Revised by A. Cleveland Coxe. Vol. 1 of *Ante-Nicene Fathers.* New York: Christian Literature, 1885.

Jackson, Blomfield. *Early Church Classics: St. Polycarp, Bishop of Smyrna.* Reprint. New York: Andesite, 2017.

Justin Martyr. *The First and Second Apologies.* Mahwah, NJ: Paulist, 1997.

Kieckhefer, Richard. *Magic in the Middle Ages.* 2nd ed. New York: Cambridge University Press, 2000.

Longenecker, Dwight. "Arianism Today." Patheos, Jan. 2, 2012. https://www.patheos.com/blogs/standingonmyhead/2012/01/arianism-today.html.

MacArthur, John. *The Gospel According to Jesus.* Grand Rapids: Zondervan, 2008.

McDonald, Lee Martin, and James A. Sanders. *The Canon Debate.* Peabody, MA: Hendrickson, 2002.

Moore, Edward. "Gnosticism." Internet Encyclopedia of Philosophy, n.d. https://www.iep.utm.edu/gnostic/.

Moorhouse, Roger. *Killing Hitler: The Plots, the Assassins, and the Dictator Who Cheated Death.* New York: Bantam, 2007.

The Nicene Constantinopolitan Creed. MIT, n.d. http://web.mit.edu/ocf/www/nicene_creed.html.

Okholm, Dennis L., and Timothy R. Phillips. *Four Views on Salvation in a Pluralistic World.* Grand Rapids: Zondervan, 1995.

Phillips, Jonathan. *Ancient Roads from Christ to Constantine.* Austin, TX: Galan Productions, 2015. DVD.

Polycarp. *The Sacred Writings of Saint Polycarp.* Loschberg, Germ.: Jazzybee, 2016.

Poncelet, A. "St. Irenaeus." New Advent, n.d. From vol. 8 of *The Catholic Encyclopedia* (New York: Appleton, 1910). http://www.newadvent.org/cathen/08130b.htm.

Roberts, Alexander, et al., eds. *Nicene and Post-Nicene Fathers.* 2nd ser. Peabody, MA: Hendrickson, 1996.

Ryken, Leland. "Who Is Wisdom in Proverbs 8?" Christian Research Institute, June 9, 2009. From *Christian Research Journal,* volume 27, number 2 (2004). Article ID: D1504. https://www.equip.org/articles/ Who Is Wisdom in Proverbs 8/.

Tobisch, David. "Who Published the New Testament?" *Free Inquiry* 28 (2007/2008) 30–33.

Wingren, Gustaf. "St. Irenaeus, Bishop of Lyon." *Encyclopaedia Britannica,* Oct. 28, 2021. Revised by the Editors of Encyclopedia Britannica; last updated by Melissa Petruzzello. https://www.britannica.com/biography/Irenaeus.

9 781666 757606